GW01471588

1953: Life in Worle

Snapshot of a Village

Raye Green

I have included in this little book everything I could discover about Worle in 1953, from politics to carnival. I hope it will enable you to re-live a happy year of your life. The diary at the end is for you to add personal memories.

Published by Honey Pot Press
2 The Dell, Worle
BS22 9LZ
www.honey-pot-press.co.uk

This edition 2011

ISBN 978-0-9569752-2-5

Contents

Why 1953?

When a small group of us formed the Worle History Society early in 2009 one of the priorities we talked about was the need to preserve, as far as possible, memories of our much loved village. We were aware of just how easy it is to lose first hand information about life in days gone by,

So, I suggested that maybe we could research and write up a 'snapshot year' which would give future generations an idea of what life used to be like in Worle. I thought of 1953 for several reasons. Firstly, I remembered it, which I hoped would help. Secondly, it was Coronation year; so many people would have clear memories. Thirdly, it was a significant year for Worle and its inhabitants in another, sad way. It was the year when the Council decided to allow building to commence between Milton and Worle.

So, 1953 is a huge turning point: the last year that Worle had a real village identity, completely separate from that of surrounding areas.

We all agreed that this would be one of our projects, and since it was my silly idea, and I really wanted to do it, I volunteered. Luckily I have had lots of help and some major contributions from friends old and new. I owe a particular debt to people who have contributed photographs from their family albums, especially the weddings. St Martin's Junior School allowed us to look at and copy minutes, registers and pictures and the Church gave me access to their records. Somerset Records Office supplied details of burials, weddings and baptisms; sporting memorabilia was given by Johnnie Tucker, Eric Maggs and others; generously, I have been let into homes, given coffee and allowed to question folk for hours. I have been trusted to take precious keepsakes away to be copied. Eric Tyler sorted out all his collection about the Methodist Chapel. Local historians with years of experience have helped willingly to fill in the gaps. Brian Austin sends me notes and telephones me each time he thinks of something. Oh, and how glad I am that the old copies of the Mercury are there for all to use for research.

I have re-lived a year of my childhood and I think it is time to share the memories. If there are errors or omissions, I am sorry. Please let me know and perhaps there will be a second edition.

So, here goes!

The Wider Context

On New Year's Day in the year 1953 the world, as we knew it in Worle, was recovering from the Second World War. Elizabeth II was Head of State, following the premature death of King George V1, but the new Queen was not yet crowned and people often forgot to sing 'God Save the Queen' instead of 'God Save the King'; Winston Churchill was back as Prime Minister. He lost the 1945 general election, but recaptured power in 1951; the age of austerity was softening and rationing was becoming a thing of the past.

In the wider world, away from our cosy village, things were happening. These are just a few examples of major events that year, to give us an idea before we start:

February 3rd   Severe flooding on the east coast of England

March 5th   Stalin died

March 14th   Khrushchev emerged as leader of the USSR

March 24th   Queen Mary died

March 25th   Polio vaccination announced

April 8th   Mau Mau leader Jomo Kenyatta jailed

May 29th   Hillary and Tensing reached summit of   Everest

June 2nd   Coronation of H.M. Queen Elizabeth II

June 18th   Egyptian republic proclaimed

July 27th   Korean War armistice signed

August 14th   Soviet hydrogen bomb test

November 21st   Piltdown skull exposed as a hoax

December 23rd   Former KGB chief, Beria, was executed.

I thought it would paint a picture of a softer, kinder world, but this list is a pretty mixed bag, erring on the negative, just as now.

So what about sport? The football world cup was held by Uruguay. The FA cup final was played between Blackpool [4] and Bolton Wanderers [3], Cambridge won the boat race and Pinza, ridden by Gordon Richards, triumphed in the Derby.

This was the first year of an official HIT Parade top ten, and Frankie Laine was king with 3 different hits from April until Christmas, of which 'I believe' was the most popular. Marilyn Monroe gave all other women a complex.

All this can be picked up in half an hour of quick research, but finding out what life was like in Worle, I have discovered, takes rather longer.

What the village looked like

Arguably, the area which we called the village of Worle could be said, in 1953, to mean 26 streets. Of course, there were little by-ways and lanes, but when I came to draw a street map of the village as it was then, I felt that 26 was about the right number. Should we include New Bristol Road?   I suppose so; and what about the little crescent which was then Preanes Green? The best way to describe what we mean by 'Worle' is to look at map. You will see that we began with Spring Hill in the west and finished with Kewstoke Road in the north-east. The High Street from end to end and the roads that radiate from it form a large part of the village and New Bristol Road – with the emphasis on the word 'new' - is a firm punctuation mark to the south. I do ask myself whether Old Bristol Road should appear on the map, but there will always be discussions on these finer points.

There is also a difficulty with the accurate placing of buildings on a map. The Ordnance Survey produces new versions of maps in response to considerable change, so I have been unable to trace an official map for 1953. The ordnance map for c. 1936 provides some guidance as to the buildings existing then, but also presents us with a tantalising 17 year gap. However it does give us a sense of scale which may be valuable and some clues as to the ownership of land.

Worle in the late 1930s – the nearest available
date

The village grew up on the south side of its hill – an odd looking lump, especially when viewed from the M5 motorway. In 1953, the High Street had established itself as the main commercial street. Housing in the village was varied. Many houses were built with the beautiful stone from the quarry in Kewstoke Road and this grey stone also provided the walls that surrounded precious gardens. These walls supported the bright purple flowers with crisp vivid green foliage which exploited any crevice it could find and made the late Spring such a joy. The stone houses, still such a feature of the area, came in many styles, from small terraced cottages, through Victorian villas to double fronted detached places, but some new building was creeping in. Annandale Avenue was lined with modern architecture, bungalows, no less, and Hill Road had more bungalows and semi-detached council housing. I suppose the icing on the cake were the cottages, some tiled, others thatched and the two Georgian houses, elegant and cream. The Maltings, a cul-de-sac off the High Street, had prefabricated homes which temporarily replaced buildings damaged or destroyed by the bombing. This little road had a wonderful community atmosphere and was fascinating to me as a child.

The streets were almost all adopted and surfaced by the Town Council but there were some exceptions. Hawthorn Hill was a rough stone road with wild hedgerows; Hill Road East had a similar stone surface and just faded out. Several of the small dead end streets finished with a patch of untended grass and a rhyne. The street lighting was provided by gentle gas lamps, the lamp stands were painted silver, except for the wider bases, which were green. When they were lit, there was an eerie glow. Work had started on the installation of electric street lights, but was not complete. Telegraph poles ran along the length of the main streets and the stays that secured these were often located in front

11

gardens. A twisted cable would run from the top of the pole at an angle and was sunk in concrete to keep the pole upright. We had one of these stays in our garden and were paid a shilling [5p] a year by the electricity board for the inconvenience.

The postman needed to be very familiar with the village as many of the dwellings were known by house names and were not numbered. In longer streets, like the High Street, this must have been a difficulty for anyone new. Our house was enigmatically called 'Windsor', next door was 'Sandringham' followed by 'Balmoral'. Other names were less pretentious like 'The Roses', 'The Laurels' and so forth. Some houses have kept their names and simply added a number, but many have been forgotten.

St Martin's Church, the Methodist Chapel, the Church Hall, four public houses, the Century Club, a dozen or so shops, the recreation ground and three schools provided community spaces where the people of Worle met daily to gossip, laugh, cry, exchange ideas and conduct business. All very satisfactory as it was, but greatly enhanced by the mainstay of the village: agriculture.

Worle could more or less feed itself in 1953. There were farms in and around the village, market gardens too numerous to count and gardens where vegetables grew and chickens pecked. Dairy cows wandered between fields and milking sheds twice a day. We did, of course, have some exotic food, like bananas and oranges, but the basic diet was fruit and vegetables in season, pork from local pigs, beef from local cattle, chicken...... you've got the hang of it. The market gardeners sold their own produce to the villagers or to local shops, and allotment holders sold or swapped their surplus. The bread was all made at home or in local bakeries, the cider in the pubs was local. If the rest of the world had disappeared, Worle would have survived.

Obviously, with all this production going on, we were well blessed with fields, orchards and open spaces, all criss-crossed with the characteristic rhynes. These drainage ditches were essential to keep the land dry enough to be workable, and were a delight to generations of local children. The seasons of the year ruled the lives of many of the people and harvest festivals were a genuine celebration of the fruits of people's labour. Winning classes at the Horticultural Show meant good business for the growers for another year.

Getting about was different then. We walked mostly; some people had bicycles with baskets on the front to carry shopping, and a few businesses had vans to deliver goods or carry equipment. The minimal amount of traffic meant that there were no zebra crossings, mini roundabouts, traffic lights, yellow lines, white lines or parked cars. We did have a keep left sign at the junction of High Street with Milton Road. This modern phenomenon was referred to with some awe in our household. Like many small towns, or big villages, Worle was way behind the great commercial and industrial cities and towns, where traffic lights had been common since the late 1920s, roundabouts were regular features and even the first zebra crossing had striped roads for the past two years.

There were some cars in Worle, but these were rare enough to make collecting car numbers a gentle pastime and there were nearly as many tractors. The rag and bone man still used a horse and cart, as did some of the farms, but 'buses ruled. The green, number 40 'buses went up and down the High Street every ten minutes each way, stopping 3 times on their way along, turning round at the bottom of the Scaurs and making their way back to Weston – the metropolis.

3635

So, what about the people? Without the help of census figures for the time, which will not be available for nearly 50 years, I can only make an educated guess, based on history, about the population size of Worle. We know that, in the Borough Council elections in May of 1953, there were 4,519 electors in Milton and Worle ward. All this really tells us, is that in Milton and Worle combined 4,519 people were over the age of 21 and eligible to vote. If we say that half of these people lived in Worle – a bit of an assumption – it suggests that about 2,250 people of 21 years and older, lived in the village. A study of the statistics from censuses up to 1901 suggests that almost 50% of the population of the village was under 20 years of age at each 10 year interval between censuses. Maybe this was still the case in the 1950s, in which case perhaps four and a half thousand people lived in our 26 streets – more of a town than a village?

A large proportion of the population was supported by farming and horticulture, but small retail businesses also thrived and construction was enjoying something of a resurgence following the war. New homes were in demand and craftsmen as well as suppliers were doing better. Some of the men left the village on the buses or on their bicycles, to work in Weston, or in another village. I dare say some worked in Bristol, and travelled by train, but I didn't know anyone this brave. The local railway service, the buses, Fussell's rubber factory, Forsey's [which was something to do with pigs and offal] employed their fair share of the men. Fewer of the women worked. There were shop jobs, of course, and the laundries provided opportunities, but most of the women had their work cut out to look after hearth and home, children, chickens, vegetable gardens and most of all, their husbands.

As in all communities, there was also a need for the professions and for public service provision. The three schools, doctors' practices, solicitors' offices and even one estate agent meant that white collar jobs were around, if rare. And then there were the places of worship. St Martin's Church in particular, was capable of flexing its muscles, as we shall see.

Throughout the population, whether blue collar or white, there was a predictable sameness of appearance, which makes it nye on impossible to identify individuals from old photographs. The men seemed to wear long mackintoshes and trilby hats whenever they needed to look at all tidy and this uniform applied from a young age –early 20s anyway. Men in their late teens were a mystery to the rest of us, since they were always away on national service for at least two years, and they came back sorted out and conforming, for the most part. The women were apparently not interested in fashion, few wore makeup of any kind and clothes were mostly lacking colour and style. It was essential for females, who could no longer be called girls, to wear a hat out of doors and none would have gone into a Church bare-headed.

Men ran the show. They had societies and organisations galore, which provided fun and recreation. The women were little helpers, who sometimes had their 'ladies' branches' of established societies. These women entertained themselves by fund raising with 'sales of work' or making tea or washing the kit, etc, etc. I had no idea at the time, but these facts meant that my mother stuck out like a sore thumb. She worked full time teaching in Hutton, so set off first thing on her bike and returned at tea time, she wore lipstick and powder at all times, she worried about her hair [always curled] and her clothes, she started things like the chapel choir and Sunday School and meddled in politics. She thought men were at best her equal and at worst hopeless. It was years later that I realised that the other women thought her 'the limit'.

So this was Worle in a very tiny nutshell, run by public spirited landowners and villagers, dictated to by the church, governed by Weston Borough Council's conservatives and by Somerset County Council's conservatives, ruled by Winston Churchill's conservative post-war government in Westminster and reigned over by Her Majesty Queen Elizabeth II. No wonder we had a Ratepayers' Association!

Politics and Politicians

Sir Ian Leslie Orr-Ewing, M.P.

The early 1950s were still permeated by the traditions and expectations of a pre-war society and this was certainly true in an agricultural village like Worle. The most influential people in the village were mostly, but not all, men.

1953 must have dawned fair for the Member of Parliament for the constituency of Weston-super-Mare, which included Worle. Ian Leslie Orr-Ewing was born in Ayr on 4th June 1893, one of a line of career politicians, all Conservatives. On the last day of 1952 he retired, a commoner, to his bed at Christon Old Rectory, near Axbridge where he, Mrs. Helen Orr-Ewing, nee Gibbs, and their one daughter of the marriage had lived for 15 years, and he awoke on January 1st 1953 a Knight of the Realm, having been elevated by the young Queen in her New Year's Honours List.   He had been elected to represent the constituency in 1934, following the death of the previous incumbent, Lord Erskine, and remained our MP until his death on 27th April, 1958.   His majority in the 1951 General Election was an impressive 14,543 votes.

Considering his lineage and the longevity of his membership of the House of Commons, it was surprising to find that more was written about Sir Ian following his death than in his lifetime. The obituaries in our archives speak of a *'distinguished career'* and *'an MP who was respected by all'*. The Bristol Evening Post remembers that he *'Spent himself generously in public and political life'*.

As with all people in public life, opinions of Sir Ian vary. Even today I spoke to two men who had both met him and had completely opposite attitudes. One said he was a gentleman, well-spoken and every inch a politician, someone to respect. The other said that local people hated him, that he cared nothing for the constituency and its people and did little to help them. He was stuck up and politics was not a calling, it was a career. The only way out of this dilemma is to stick to the facts.

SIR IAN ORR-EWING

The picture which accompanies the Bristol Evening World report on the day after his death shows a greying, distinguished man. The photograph is of his left profile, which begs the question, is this his good eye? Sir Ian was blinded in one eye in a childhood accident, a misfortune which later blighted his hopes of a career in the Royal Navy. Instead, after Harrow and Oxford, he trained to become an architect and later served in the Great War with the Royal Scots Fusiliers, and was wounded in action. The only full length portraits I have been able to trace are in uniform and bemedalled, looking very stiff and formal, as one would expect. They were both photographs taken in 1939, when he was already a Member of Parliament.

How does someone born in Ayr relate to the problems of a seaside town in Somerset, I wonder, and particularly, how does he begin to understand a village like Worle? Well, Ayr is a seaside town on the west coast of Britain, so maybe that helped, but I doubt if he had much understanding of a West Country village, where the primary concern was raising cash for the Coronation celebrations, sorting out the obnoxious smell from Forsey's factory and retrieving the Cricket Club's stolen tea things. In any case Worle was one small corner of a large, sprawling constituency and drew little attention compared with its much larger neighbour, Weston-super-Mare.

A trawl through Hansard for 1953 only uncovered two mentions that are of any significance of the man who represented us. Mostly he was paired with a Labour MP so that neither of them had to attend and vote. However, he did speak twice in 1953. The first time was on 30th January in a debate on the Sunday Observance bill to which he contributed 34 words as follows:

'Is the hon. Member suggesting that Sunday political meetings, which are not organised by those on this side of the House, are commercial enterprises? Is not that a new conception of a political meeting?'

He voted against the bill, thereby helping to change our Sundays for ever.

The second time he was roused to speak was in February on the 13th of the month during the Criminal Justice Amendment Bill, when again he voted NO. This time he said

'Would my right hon. and learned Friend in any event be prepared to undertake to examine the methods which are now used to bring to the attention of those who occupy the bench in any capacity, the records of those who have passed through their hands after sentence? Secondly, would he also institute an enquiry to discover whether it would be advisable or not to give publicity to second and further offenders who come before the juvenile court?'

The Mercury has failed to turn up any mention of Orr-Ewing during the year, and it is his obituaries that tell us that he had owned a home in the constituency since 1938, when he had bought Christon Old Rectory – not in Weston and certainly not in Worle! It is not apparent how often he visited Weston, spoke at meetings or held surgeries. People were much more in awe of politicians then and would not have expected to have any contact with them. Little would have been known about their political interests or their backgrounds by most of their constituents.

Orr-Ewing was, in fact, well informed on a variety of topics. He took an active interest in the Central African Republic question as a member of the Bledisloe Commission and was much respected by his fellow MPs in this regard. He made a speech [not in the House] on the subject which was alluded to several times in a parliamentary debate in 1953, although he did not speak himself. Then there was the debate on the Monopolies and Restrictive Practices Bill, during which Orr-Ewing was mentioned again. Perhaps the greatest bee in his bonnet was the campaign for the use of Home Grown Timber, so maybe it is as well that he didn't pop along to Worle too often or he might have had his eye on our woods. Still, it does suggest some advanced green credentials for the mid twentieth century.

The people of Worle and the rest of the area obviously turned out to support Orr-Ewing regularly during his twenty odd years as MP. Even when Labour swept to victory in 1945, he still kept his seat with a respectable majority of 10,178. *'The blue rinse brigade will always turn out'* was a favourite saying locally, and was true.

There is anecdotal evidence of Orr-Ewing making an effort to get to know the people of Worle some years previously. In 1949 the staff of Worle Secondary School contacted the MP and organised a day trip to the House of Commons. Peter Snook remembers the pupils saving a few bob regularly at school until they had the 49/6d [approximately £2.50] needed to pay for the outing. Pete thinks they went by train because a journey by road was a long, drawn out business in those pre-motorway days. They may have caught the train at Weston station or at Milton Halt, and were met in Parliament by Orr-Ewing, who took them into the Commons, where they sat on the green benches. Orr-Ewing was well dressed, very smart indeed by Worle standards and spoke with a Scottish accent. He was regarded with some awe and it is interesting that he is remembered so clearly 60 years later. The Bristol Evening World considered that *'his courtesy and natural friendliness and his able manner at public meetings endeared him to many........'*, which confirms Peter's memories.

Westminster Hall also made an impression on the children of Worle, but the greatest memory of the day was the drinking water in a cafe where they had lunch. The water was in a jug and the children poured it out and started to drink – but not for long. It was dreadful stuff, certainly not drinkable and nothing like the water at home. When they complained to the waitress she said, 'Well we drink it', and that was that.

Perhaps the memory of this day helped to maintain the Conservative vote in the village. Certainly the evidence suggests that Orr-Ewing was supported locally not only by the grass roots but also by a large number of Conservative Councillors on Weston Borough Council.

Borough Council: Milton and Worle Ward

The ward that covered our village was Milton and Worle ward and was one of six in the Borough. Each ward was represented by three councillors who were elected for a three year stint. Every May, one of the three councillors stood for re-election. This was a sensible system, since it meant that only a third of the council could be replaced at any one time and two-thirds would be experienced. Much better than 2011, when the whole council can be thrown out at one go and replaced by folk who have no clue how the systems work. Two of Worle's representatives on the Borough Council in 1953 were Conservatives and the third was an independent with conservative tendencies.

Councillors H. S. Allen and Captain James Leslie Trevitt did not have to face the electorate in 1953, only Frederick Clarence Bessell, a local chemist had the worry of re-election [or not] that May 7th. It is interesting to note that none of these three men lived in Worle. Capt. Trevitt lived at 11 Cecil Road in Weston. He had been to school in Weston and was a Sandhurst man who had seen active service in both World Wars, having been a regular in the Cheshires. Everyone professed to dislike him, but still elected him. Mrs Trevitt, as we shall learn, was a definite asset to her husband and the village.

Fred Bessell owned two chemist shops, one of which was in Worle High Street, next door to my childhood home. His business partner, Mr. [Ginger] Raikes, ran the Worle shop but I don't believe I ever set eyes on Mr. Bessell, who lived at 205 Milton Road. He had been a councillor for some time, and was standing as an independent – very brave. Mr. Bessell's independent status gave the local Conservative Association a problem – to stand against Bessell or not to stand against Bessell? The Labour party smelled the hope of a weakness and put up a candidate – a woman – Mrs Edith Livingstone, secretary of the party's local branch. This stalwart worked part time as a dinner lady at Milton School and was a delegate to the Trades Council for the National Union of Public Employees. There was just a chance she might attract a dangerous number of votes. The Tories decided on their strategy. They would not put up a candidate against Fred Bessell, whom they believed they could manipulate. The following announcement appeared in the Mercury on April 24th, 1953.

"The Conservative Association are contesting South, East, Central and Ellenborough Wards with officially adopted Conservative candidates. It was not their intention at any time to contest the Milton and Worle Ward with an official candidate, as they have no wish to split the anti-Socialist vote there – an action that would only lead to the success of the Socialist Candidate.

"The Conservative Association therefore urges all Conservatives in the Milton and Worle Ward to record their votes in favour of the retiring representative, Councillor Bessell, who is being opposed by a socialist candidate."

This appeared in the same article as the information about candidates in the other five wards and shows the paper's frightful bias, which I would have thought was illegal. There were mutterings in socialist households, including ours. It amounted to a free advertisement supplied by the newspaper. But it worked. Large numbers voted for Fred Bessell, chemist of the ward, and he won. Bessell polled 1,123 and Mrs. Livingstone 635. She might have had a good shot at it if everyone had played fair

What sort of councillor did Mr Bessell turn out to be? Did he vote with the Conservatives? The Borough Council minutes

[Weston Library] do not answer these questions, but there are clues elsewhere. Mr. Bessell was one of the managers at Worle Junior School and their minutes show that he attended a managers' meeting on Thursday 22nd January. Bear in mind that this was in the run up to the crucial election in May, and he would have needed to be seen to be involved. Further meetings of the Junior School management took place in May, July, October and December, and Mr. Bessell attended none of these, sending apologies on 3 occasions and simply not appearing on the fourth. It was a small board of managers and the constant absence of one member must have galled the others. Did they comment? Did they moan? If so, there is no mention in the minutes. Perhaps Mr. Bessell was unwell, but I think they would have minuted that. One can't help thinking that, once elected, he lost interest. So much for Independent councillors which I had always thought a good idea!

So what was Worle's status in the Borough? Well, there were, as mentioned before, 6 wards in all and Worle accounted for approximately half of one ward, so we could estimate that the village should have received about 8 or 9% of the attention of the Borough Council. Goodness knows whether the village did get its fair share of the combined brain power of the Council. Apart from full council meetings, there were regular meetings of the various committees, of which, the following discussed matters directly appertaining to Worle: Estates and Plans; Housing; Parks, Parades and Sands; Civil Defence, Public Health and Water.

During 1953 decisions directly affecting Worle were minuted on 54 occasions. These are broken down thus:

The Housing Committee made 4 decisions affecting Worle. On the 5th January they decided to decorate the 'aged persons dwellings at The Rows, Worle', spending £10 on each home. On

June 8th a compulsory purchase order was proposed for 'building sites at Worle'. October 5th saw the formal appropriation of Light Railway Land at Preanes Green and finally, on November 2nd a further Preanes Green issue arose, but a decision was deferred. They did not know what to do about discharging effluent and sewage into the rhynes and a temporary pipeline was proposed, which would last for 10 years. This is the one issue of any long term importance to Worle that was discussed by the Housing Committee in the entire year and they failed to make a decision. Oh dear. I wonder what happened to the sewage, perhaps it is better not to know.

Parks, Parades and Sands obviously affected Weston much more than Worle, so it would have been pointless for our 3 councillors to sit on this committee at first glance, but here, too, Worle was affected by 4 items. On February 23rd they decided that permission would be granted for 'usual facilities' on Worle Recreation Ground on August 3rd for the Annual Flower Show. In June the Town Clerk read a letter from Mr. Les Bull, the headmaster of Worle Junior School, requesting permission to use Grove Park for a performance of the Royal Pageant by the children. Permission was granted in principle. On July 8th a discussion took place concerning the storage of the Coronation Decorations. I suspect that these were mostly in town, but maybe Worle had some that were not privately owned. In any case, nowhere could be found to put them, so that was that. Did they go down to the tip? Finally, on August 31st, Worle Rec was mentioned again in connection with a lease for a transformer station. SWEB wanted their lease extended for 21 years. This was agreed with some provisos, increased rent and get-out clauses. And that was that for Worle and the PPS committee.

On June the 9th the Civil Defence Committee turned its collective mind to Worle for the one and only time that year. Air Raid Warning Sirens were the issue. It was reported that all sirens were now erected – how dramatic, and how odd it seems now - and SWEB were supplying the power. There was a need to install a 3-phase service at the Imperial Laundry, Worle, at a cost of £30 and a Remote Control was to be put in the Post Office Telephone Department at an annual rent of £150/8/-. This seems like a fortune for those days. Why did the 3-phase service need to be in the laundry? What was the remote control thing like? I'd love to ask my late father, who worked in the Telephone Exchange at the time.

The Public Health and Water Committee met on 28th October. One of the issues discussed was the 'burning of offal at a certain premises at Worle'. Everyone knew it was Forces factory, but the committee evidently preferred to be coy about it.

The Estate and Plans committee is awarded the gold star for paying attention to the village. About 40 issues regarding planning permission in Worle were discussed and either passed or rejected during the year. Amongst them, there are a few of special interest. Rock Cottage in Lawrence Road was declared unfit for human habitation on March 2nd. The cottage is still standing, and still lived-in over 50 years later. Permission to convert the coach house at the back of Fairfield in the High Street was turned down for lack of space; permission was also refused for semi-detached bungalows in Spring Hill, but allowed for a single detached bungalow a month later. Greenwood Road was allowed to have another dwelling, and Step-a-side in Pine hill was given the go ahead for a garage. The area still at that time referred to as 'The Splotts' was to be the site of six bungalows. Two areas in Worle

26

seem to have been referred to as 'The Splotts' over the years. In earlier times this might have meant Lawrence Road, but in 1953 would probably have referred to part of Spring Hill.

The Ratepayers' Association

The voters in the town took a great interest in the affairs of the Borough Council, which was just as well considering the lack of a natural opposition on the Council at the time. The conservatives were the vast majority so the electorate kept a close eye on them. The Ratepayers' Association met on a regular basis all over the town and at their AGM on January 28th they reported 2,915 paid up members. When it was the turn of Milton and Worle ward to host it, the Church Hall was pressed into service and meetings were well attended. Letters were often written to the Council drawing attention to matters that needed to be noted or resolved.

The weather led to some discontent! In February, the Ratepayers' Association wrote to the Council about it and the matter had to be mentioned at the Full Council meeting on February 4th. Snow clearance, or the lack of it, was at the bottom of the unhappiness and the people vented their annoyance at the inefficiency. The Council was not impressed by the complaint, dubbing it 'frivolous, unjust and unfounded'. I wonder how Mr. P. E. Culling, President of the Association, felt about that response. Frivolous, well well.

More important to most people was the 'abominable stench'. We tend, with the rose coloured glasses of nostalgia, to remember sunny days, fields of buttercups where houses now stand, catching sticklebacks and newts in the rhynes. We omit to recall the smell of burning offal which emanated from Forces factory. For some reason this always seemed worse in the Autumn, and in the October of 1953 it just became too much. The residents of Worle, via the Ratepayers' Association, decided to petition the Council to take steps to abate the nuisance. The petition was read aloud at a meeting in the Church Hall and was signed by 100 people, though Mr. M. R. Adams, who helped organise the petition said they could have collected 500 signatures if they had had the time to spare. Mr Adams was also at pains to point out that he had visited the proprietor of the factory, who was full of sympathy. Said Mr. Adams, *'He realises what everybody in Worle realises – it is a confounded nuisance.'*

The Health Committee considered the matter seriously and wrote a response saying that, 'certain improvements were being carried out at the premises which would mitigate the cause of the complaint.' Certainly things improved after a while, and eventually the stink disappeared altogether. Everyone who lived in Worle at the time recalls the smell when asked about it. Some actually say they liked it, most were relieved to be able to leave doors and windows open again. The negative headlines in the paper about 'my village' upset me as a child. Phrases like 'obnoxious smells', 'to sweeten Worle's atmosphere', 'deodorisation units' and 'abominable stench' did nothing to enhance our reputation. My family were rather laid back about the whole thing. Coming, as they did, from Ebbw Vale, a bit of burning offal was nothing compared with the sulphurous emissions from the Steel Works.

Our natural village boundaries

On top of smells, snow and effluent being tipped into the rhynes it seems that we also had a 'bottleneck'. This was situated at the junction of the Scaurs and the High Street – often called the Terminus, since the 40 buses, all double deckers, did their three-point turns at this spot. This was an interesting procedure, the passing of which I personally regret. The road narrowed dramatically by the New Inn [now the Woodspring] and created a natural boundary between the centre of the village and the rest of the world. Quite right, too. As we shall see later, this was not the only natural boundary under threat. There was a report in the Mercury which, together with the Council minutes, gives us some background information. The Council was planning to widen the road and were negotiating a swap – all right they called it an exchange – of land. They decided to pay the 'other party', who was not named, £275, surveyor's fees of 18 guineas and appropriate legal costs. Sadly, there is no record of which piece of land was exchanged, or for what, or who owned it, but the end of the village was no more and the buses drove straight around to face the other way with no intricate manoeuvres.

Truthfully, I think most people thought this was a good thing, but the Green Wedge was another matter.

On January 9th of our snapshot year the Mercury reported that the *'GREEN BELT MAY NOT BE IN DEVELOPMENT PLAN'*. This needs some explaining. At the west end of the High Street, then as now, there was a Keep Left sign. This marked the end of Worle as far as the people were concerned. There was an undeveloped area which, on the left hand side of Milton Road stretched as far as Baytree playing field, and almost as far on the right. This was the Green Wedge as it was officially called [green island to the locals] and had been protected by the 'Master Plan' for the area, agreed in the 1940s before the Town and Country Planning Act of 1947. The Master Plan was about to bite the dust, and the Development Plan was about to take over.

It was decided that the green wedge was already very small and would not be a great loss. In-filling was becoming a popular feature of town and country planning and Worle was going to be sacrificed. One major argument was the need for a new school in the area, which was proposed for part of the land. That never did happen, of course. The land was all used for housing and the separate identity of Worle, which a previous council had protected, was lost for ever.

Did the electorate realise what was happening? Did our M.P. point out the disadvantages? Why did Worle continue to vote for these people? I don't know, but I expect that there was no real understanding of what a difference it would make. My father went to the Town Hall to study the plans and discovered that even then ideas had been mooted for vast development to the north of Worle. We now know that we had little time left to be a close-knit village community, but we made the best of it for as long as it lasted.

Church Matters

There is a general belief that Sundays were very different in the mid 20th century, and of course there is considerable truth in this. Certainly the roads were not clogged with cars heading for supermarkets or DIY stores. Many people, in 1953, still kept the Sabbath holy, but not as many as you may think.

A day of rest only works for a privileged section of a farming village. The animals still needed their usual attention, so the cows were driven through the streets to be milked; the horses at the stables were still mucked out and fed, the market gardeners still needed to tend their crops. The women all got down to some serious cooking in order to produce Sunday lunch. Once the meat was in and veg prepared, it was a matter of up to your elbows in flour to supply the household with an apple pie. After dinner it took a good hour to wash up and clear away the mess.

Although most of the shops were closed for the day, there is some discussion about Prewitt's, the newsagent's shop on the south side of the High Street. This small space had been Griffin's cycle shop until Prewitt's took over. Some think it was open on Sunday mornings to sell the Sunday papers, others say it was shut and the papers were delivered. I know that if a visit to Prewitt's was possible, you would have been confronted by a nameless, little, rounded old lady sitting on a stool. Customers always helped themselves to their desired purchases and the stool lady simply took the money. She never rose to serve anyone, on account of having an artificial boot on one leg – something else I found most interesting as a child. I asked her about it one day and she told me she had had her leg chopped off, but I've no idea whether this was true.

Despite all this underground activity the village did take on a different air on Sundays. On normal week days the village was abuzz with pedestrians going about their business, but on Sundays it was almost deserted until ten o'clock, when folk began to appear in their Sunday best, the men in suits, if they had one, and the women in hats and gloves. Some of these wended their way towards the Methodist chapel in Lawrence Road, most headed towards St. Martin's Church on the hill. Of course, a few dedicated worshippers had already been to Holy Communion at St. Martin's at eight o'clock, but most were still at rest at that hour and did not emerge until the bells began to peal.

Men of the Church. Rev. Eric Vallance Cook is 3rd from the left.

Eric Vallance Cook, Vicar of Worle since 1949, greeted his congregation and presided over the services. Surprisingly, St. Martin's was very high church. Incense was always used, chanting was normal. On the occasions when I visited this Church, I was amazed by the goings–on and particularly fascinated by the vicar and choir men wearing dresses. After evening service, Vallance

Cook could be seen hurrying down Hill Road in his cassock en route to the Golden Lion for his reward of a pint of best. This was in remarkable contrast to the Methodist approach to worship, which entailed sombre suits for the men, certainly no frocks, and a complete ban on alcohol. Even the communion wine was non-alcoholic. So, Church of England folk had real wine and pretend bread and Methodists had pretend wine and real bread. Each thought the other was odd.

Worle's 'old' Vicarage had been in the High Street, a few dozen yards west of the War Memorial, but by 1953 the Vicar and his family resided in a Victorian house in Church Road, facing directly down Coronation Road, with wonderful views of the Mendips. Whilst this sounds rather lovely, it was actually a barn of a place, difficult to keep clean and maintain and impossible to heat. There was a large outbuilding at the top of the long drive, past the house. This had once been the garage but had been handed over to the First Worle Guide Company for their head quarters, so on Friday evenings at around 6.00 o'clock even the non-conformist girls penetrated the vicar's domain for the Guides' meeting. Gill Blakeman was the Guide Captain. She was a very smart spinster in her 30s and had a very stiff manner which frightened the men away. Lieutenant Perry [Lefty] redressed the balance with her comfortable, motherly approach.

Only on very rare occasions did the vicar appear to say hello to the girls and when he did, Captain would become girly and ingratiating.

Vallance Cook also visited the older children at Worle Junior School regularly, but not too often. He took a jolly approach to these visits, probably to avoid putting the children off the whole idea of attending Church. It was a good strategy; the children all liked him and believed that he liked them. He was, in fact, generally well liked and he popped up everywhere. The Junior School was a Voluntary Controlled Church of England School, so Vallance Cook had some influence over its doings and was Chairman of the Managers' Committee. This was the forerunner of the School Governors, but had a much narrower brief. Throughout 1953, he never missed a meeting and even welcomed the Managers and the candidates to his own living room for the purpose of interviewing prospective new teachers. And this on 21st December, a very busy time for a man of the Cloth.

There were times, however, when he could make his presence felt.

The Vicar versus Worle Old Boys Football Club

It was towards the end of March when trouble broke out. The village was frantically trying to raise money to celebrate the coming Coronation on June 2nd. Worle Old Boys Football club held regular comic matches in aid of charities and in this year of national pride decided to donate the proceeds to the Coronation Fund. At the same time, Vallance Cook was preparing for Easter. He would also have been concentrating on the Palm Sunday services which would include the Confirmation of twelve parishioners, an important occasion. Seven of the new Church Members were youngsters of about 13 years. Margaret Williams, Joan Tozer, Jeanette Durston and Margaret Lovell lived in Hill Road and knew each other well. Five were older, including Roy Irwin, who kept goal for Worle Old Boys.

On Saturday 28th March Worle Old Boys' programme was published and available to buy at the price of 3d [the same as a bag of chips]. These programmes are beautifully produced and a source of great joy to a History Society, but this one was a peach. I quote:

'Looking at our forthcoming attractions we sincerely hope you will put two dates in your diary as definitely matches to see. Firstly on Good Friday K.O. 11.00 our ground will be the setting for an epic clash between the Coronation Rangers and the Smashers. For your information the Rangers is a team of all stars selected with great care from the ladies of the Club. The Smashers, I am afraid consisting of mere males, is also chosen from members of the Club and Committee. Referee is our well known Mr Tom Pemberthy [may he keep the peace] so roll up and see the 'weaker sex' get their own back. The match is being played in aid of the Worle Coronation Celebrations Fund'.

In addition to this announcement notices were posted around the village. The Vicar noticed. He was not a happy Easter bunny. Vallance Cook took up his pen and addressed his thoughts to the club secretary, Tom Pemberthy, thus:

'I have been horrified to read in this evening's Mercury that the Football Club has organised a comic football match in support of the Coronation Fund to take place on Good Friday at 11 a.m. Not only is this farce arranged for a day when Christian people everywhere are commemorating the Passion of our Lord, but at a time when many services will be in progress.'

One can't help thinking that the big mistake W.O.B. made was to set themselves up in competition with the Church. The football match was bound to win; Vallance Cook knew it and was certain to be upset.

He continued:

'To make matters worse, I understand that some of the young people connected with St. Martin's Church have been enlisted as players, thus depriving them of the means of performing their religious duties on this day. As a piece of callous blasphemy this fixture is unparalleled in Worle'.

This was indeed very strong language. There is no doubt the Vicar was cross. Tom Pemberthy, bless him, was taken aback by this letter, and rapidly contacted the W.O.B. committee, who agreed to postpone the game.

Far from just speaking his mind, which would have been understandable, Vallance Cook had threatened the Football Club as follows:

*'I can only assume that the committee has acted without a proper sense of responsibility in organising fun and games at the most solemn season of the year, and the repercussions on the Coronation celebrations themselves are bound to be serious, for if money is accepted by the Coronation Committee from such a deplorable source there is no doubt that the Christian organisations, which have so far played an active part will feel the necessity of withdrawing from future participation. **Neither will the Church Hall be available to the Football Club for its social events of the next season.'***

The village was in uproar and rifts were appearing between the Church and everyone else. Even the congregation at the Methodist Chapel thought the Vicar had lost all sense of proportion. The trouble was made worse by the knowledge that the comic match and its timing had been agreed by the Coronation

Committee, of which Vallance Cook was a member. He had skipped the relevant meeting. The chairman of the committee, Les Bull, headmaster of the Church of England Junior School, had supported the match.

The vicar knew he had made a tactical error, and in an effort to make amends, actually made matters worse. Having heard that the match was postponed until another date [May 15th] he said he would have supported it being played on the afternoon of Good Friday. This was very odd, particularly since the services planned for the day at St. Martin's were advertised in the Mercury thus:

Notice, it says 'Good Friday: three hours Liturgy 12 noon to 3 p.m. So why would the afternoon be OK, but not the morning?

In the Mercury report of the whole debacle, published on April 10th, we are told that the vicar later said he was quite sure the club did not intend a blasphemy and he did not think anything would have been said if it had been an ordinary football match, '*it was the fact of having the carnival* [code for the men dressing in drag and the girls in football kit] *– and in the morning. Some of my Sunday School teachers had even been enlisted to take part.*'

Only a handful of people thought that Vallance Cook was right. Most thought he had put a dampener on a good idea, which would have been great fun. It was pointed out in conversation that he went to work and to the pub in a dress and no-one minded that. When the game was played, in May, it was reported at length in the Mercury without a mention of the vicar who had offered to play to make up for the row! Five hundred people attended the match and the Coronation celebrations would have been much poorer without the money raised. It is not known how many were in the congregation for the 3 hours liturgy on Good Friday.

Path through the Churchyard used for walking.

Only one week after the Mercury 'blew the gaffe' about the Comic Football plans, the report of a Church meeting appeared in the same publication and it became obvious that there was more trouble.

Mr G. R. Parker, who lived in a detached stone house at the corner of The Scaurs and High Street, where Lloyds Bank now stands, had a complaint to make. He stated that:

'a number of people are making a right-of-way through the Churchyard and using it as a public footpath'.

He was upset because children used the path to 'fetch fish and chips and things like that'. This amazed us all, since in truth we did think of it as a public footpath, and we only walked along it. Mr Parker was also cross because the Junior School used the path to walk the children down to the Church Hall for their mid-day meal. 'It is sacred ground', said Mr. Parker. In fact, many of the children went home to lunch and didn't experience this daily march. Perhaps Mr. Parker thought the vicar was on a bit of a roll after the football arguments, and would back him up. In fact, the opposite was the case. Vallance Cook was on the defensive in the village, and said it was more convenient for the children to use the Church path. A motion to stop the school using the path was defeated.

Mr Parker was normally a friendly, likeable chap but I wonder if the proposed road widening scheme at the junction where he lived had upset his equilibrium. Perhaps he was feeling put upon.

The meeting moved on to other matters. The light at the lynch gate War Memorial had been removed in 1939, and it was decided to ask the Borough Council to re-instate it. No trace of this can be found in the Borough Council minutes. The Church Council was requested to install a water tap in the lower Churchyard. It strikes me that all these mod-cons were likely to increase the traffic on the Church path. As it was, a lovely white nanny goat was always tethered next to the path by the kissing gate and was a huge attraction to local children, since she would eat anything, even brown paper, and was much loved.

At the same meeting, which I believe was an annual affair, the vicar said that he thought there were about 200 active members of the Church, and 50 weekly communicants. As an expression of thanks to the Vicar and Mrs Cook it was decided to install a hot water system in the Vicarage.

The nitty-gritty of the meeting went as follows;

Mr A S Tripp was reappointed Vicar's warden for the 15th year, Mr. Lutley was re-elected as people's warden, Mr. C. Griffin became magazine secretary [so there must have been a parish magazine] and three people were sent off to represent the Parish on the Church Council, Miss Spencer, Miss Davidson and Mr. N. Barr. No mention was made of Eli George, which is odd.

During the year, £170 had been spent on decorating the Church Hall. This seems like a great deal of money for the time, especially when compared with the £10 spent by the council on each of the aged persons dwellings in The Rows. Still, with folk celebrating their marriages with a reception there, and the children eating their dinners, the Brownies meeting on Tuesdays and Worle Old Boys having to be threatened with no more socials there, I expect it was well spent.

The area around the Church Hall was pretty much wild. Shrubs, bushes, brambles and stingers abounded. Later that April the Brownies were 'allowed' to clear some of the ground ready for the planting of red, white and blue bedding plants. In fact, the photo shows  the hopelessness of the task. I suspect that adults were sneaked in later to finish the job. However it was achieved, the flowers were planted and bloomed merrily all that summer.

We can see from the stripes on the sleeves that Gill Cumine was the Sixer and Margaret Humphries the Seconder. Jenny Vaughan still gardens madly and lives in the house behind the bush on the left of the picture.

History made at Worle Church

Autumn brought the Harvest Festival celebrations and St. Martin's excelled itself. Headlines in the Mercury of October 2nd read: 'History was made at Worle Church' and went on 'First Ceremony of its kind since Reformation'.

The service took place on Sunday 27th September at Evensong and was officially designated a 'High Celebration of Holy Eucharist'. The very fact that the service took place indicates how High Church St. Martin's was in the 1950s. It had been over 300 years since this ceremony had been celebrated. The 16th century Reformation was a movement for the reform of abuses in the Roman Church ending in the establishment of the Reformed and Protestant Churches. The ceremony in question was essentially a Roman Catholic service, not used since Tudor times and as such, would have been conducted partially, if not wholly, in Latin. It attracted a great deal of attention and filled the Church to capacity. The provision of extra seating proved to be inadequate and every space was taken up, even the belfry.

Fortunately extra help had been brought in, so Vallance Cook was aided by Brocklesby Davis, ex-vicar of Cannington, Rev. L.A.B. White, Vicar of St. Saviour's, and 160 parishioners took communion in the course of the celebrations. Two local lads were taperers: Master R. Kingsbury and Master R. Hancock.

All these good folk were surrounded by the loveliness of Harvest Home, which the congregation had provided on the Saturday. Sunday School children took gifts to be given to the sick and needy. It must have been quite a day.

Ebenezer: The Methodist Chapel

Half way up Lawrence Road, on the right hand side, stood The Methodist Chapel, which had been given the name Ebenezer but some Dickensian sole. It was every inch a Victorian Chapel and non-conformity reigned. Whereas the Church was full of pomp and ceremony, the chapel was simple in its decoration, organisation and the nature of its services.

There were, and still are, yellow steps up to the double doors and then a little entrance with a table and a notice board. Two inner doors led into the chapel itself, which was usually painted cream, but sometimes pale blue. The light oak pews were arranged in 3 sections and were plain and identical to one another. At the front was the huge pipe organ on the left, an elaborate pulpit in the middle and the choir stalls on the right. This array actually looked rather impressive. Above the entrance doors was a first floor gallery, which was reached by a staircase that went up from the entrance porch. The children in the congregation loved the gallery and used to sneak up there to witness weddings, unobserved. There were no carpets or stone slab floors, just linoleum in a dull shade of brown. The absence of stained glass windows allowed the space to be flooded with light.

The rest of the building consisted of a Schoolroom which opened off the Chapel on the south side, and a kitchen beyond that. There was a lavatory, but it was in an impossible state, and anyone desperate ran down to the Lamb Inn – a cause of some amusement, since Methodists were supposed to be teetotal and disapproved of public houses.

Despite its austerity, this chapel was loved by its congregation and was used almost every day of the week.

On Sundays the minister, Reverend Arthur Tuley, or one of a panel of lay preachers, would preside over the services. Morning service began at 11.00 a.m. and generally concluded by 12.15: a practical sort of arrangement, since the women would put the meat in the oven before they went out and rushed off to 'do the veg' after the service. The service was simple; an opening hymn was followed by a Bible reading, then the second hymn and the 'Notices'. During the third hymn the children left the Chapel through a little door by the choir stalls and went to the School Room with their Sunday School teachers. Meanwhile, the adults settled down to an inspiring [or tedious] sermon. The concluding hymn rounded things off.

The best part of the whole process was the 'Notices', delivered every week by George Fry, a lovely chap who was afflicted with a severe stammer and a broad Somerset accent, all topped off with an ability to spray the entire congregation when he spoke. Everyone was fascinated but no one ever knew what was happening during the week and no one would sit within range of the spray at the front of the Chapel.

Evening service was at 6.30 p.m. and generally poorly attended. Holy Communion was celebrated monthly at morning service - Methodists did not believe in overdoing anything.

For the rest of the week the School Room was used for a range of activities, including: women's fellowship, Bible reading, youth club, choir practice, sales of work, social events of all kinds, Harvest supper, Dutch auctions of the produce, meetings of the Trustees, and so on. In April 1953 a Coronation Bazaar was held. There were the usual stalls, bottles, handiwork, cakes, second-hand goods and a handkerchief girl. Afternoon teas were available, but the men's stall surpassed itself. It was adorned with Cherry

Blossom from white to pink to deep red and was riveting in its beauty. A picture of it even made the Mercury. What a triumph.

The hall and all these goings-on were overseen by Jim Harris, unofficial caretaker, who lived at 'Tower View' at the top of the Scaurs with his wife, Lilly and his mother-in-law, the redoubtable Mrs. Fry.

Anniversaries were celebrated with vigour, especially the Chapel Anniversary in October and the Sunday School Anniversary in the Spring.   Both of these events were marked by the participation of almost the whole congregation. The choir always learned a new anthem, those who were good enough would give renditions on their own or in a duet. The children would act out little scenes or would recite suitable poems with worthy messages. Throughout the whole, Audrey Milliner would thump the organ, sometimes with more energy than others, depending on her condition. Audrey lived in Lawrence Road and liked to drop in at the Lamb Inn on her way to Chapel, not always to use the lavatory. So much for abstinence.

Many of the congregation attended several times during the week as well as on Sundays, so that the building was a place for social gatherings as much as for worship and the people became extended family, not acquaintances. If it snowed – it did sometimes in those days – half the congregation would turn up early for morning service, to clear the steps before Miss Ruberry and Miss Parker, the much revered oldies, arrived.

The Sunday School outings were a big attraction, and considered to be better than those organised by St. Martin's, so that as an outing approached, attendance at Sunday School would rise for a few weeks and St. Martin's would drop off, but nobody seemed to mind this strategy. Occasionally attendance prizes were actually won by children who were really Church of England. Religious tolerance seemed easy then.

Worle Old Boys Football Club

Sport of all kinds played a major role in the life of the men in Worle, but it must be acknowledged that football was the game that absorbed the attention of the most people. Of course, some villagers were avid followers of National League clubs, and filled out their Pools coupon every week. Saturday tea time would see the men earnestly listening to the football results on the wireless, praying for their permutation to bear fruit. At the same time, their vain wives were sitting in a hairdresser's chair, having their own perms attended to. Apart from this national interest, local football and its supporters were at the heart of the community.

In the 1950s, Worle Old Boys were at their zenith. To give us some idea of how important WOBs were, let's consider the figures. There were four teams, each of eleven players, plus substitutes, so that gives us at least 50 active players. The committee took up another half dozen or so, perhaps more, and each time the First Eleven played one of their Somerset Senior League games 500 supporters would turn out to watch them. Add to this the managers of each team and the coaches and there must have been 600 people, or a fifth of the population, involved in WOB activities on a regular basis.

Besides the First Eleven, there were 3 other decent teams. The Second Eleven were members of the Weston and Suburban League; the Third Eleven [called the Reserves] played reserve teams from other clubs and to cap it all there was a Youth Team that played in the Junior League.

Fortunately, Eric Maggs is a mine of valuable anecdotal information and a source of sets of programmes, which he trustingly allowed me to borrow. Eric and his friend Dennis Urch both began playing for the club's Youth Team when they were 13 years old. This team was officially the Under 18s, but with so many young men abroad 'fighting the Germans away', the boys started football early. Even in 1953, the lads in their late teens were doing National Service, so there was a gap to be filled by the younger boys.

Every Friday, when the Mercury was published, there was a column devoted to the doings of Worle Old Boys. Presumably the detail, perhaps the entire text, was supplied by the Programme Secretary, George Burnham. George was indeed a treasure, not just for his dedication and reliability, but for his wonderful prose. This was a feature not only of the Mercury reports but of the Club Notes which graced the programme each Saturday. George handed out praise and criticism with equal flare for language, as is demonstrated by this extract from the first programme for 1953, published on January 10th.

'Today for our first home game of 1953, we welcome Shepton Mallet and are confident that we will have the usual hard fought, exciting match with our opponents.

'Our last home game against Bristol City Nomads was without doubt our most demoralising performance this season. Although our opponents were a useful side, it was chiefly our bad play which lost two points. The Nomads, from the first whistle, adopted tactics to suit conditions, swinging the ball about in long cross passes and were never found standing still with the ball, but were always on the move. Once again, our lads, instead of making the ball do the work and keep the game, preferred to play close football and consequently were constantly fighting against the conditions of a heavy pitch'

So much for the First X1's efforts. In contrast, the 3rd X1 were in favour:

'Once again we must offer sincere congratulations to our youthful 3rd X1 who took five points out of six in three Christmas games, following up with a 7-1 victory over a strong Langford Rovers side last Saturday. Keep it up, lads.'

Luckily, the first X1 game against Shepton Mallet was a roaring success. The WOB's 6-2 win was reported with enthusiasm in the Mercury. 'Worle Returns to Form' was the headline. '......so convincing that a double-figured record would not have flattered them...'

This small reproduction of the programme is designed to give a flavour of the time and of the quality of the weekly publication. The team names are in the centre square and feature many well known local families: R. Gibbins, Burnham, Hutchings, W. Durston, N. Baker, D. Urch, Herries, Langdale, Williams, Maggs, Lane.

Maggs, Urch, Hutchins and Durston all lived in Kewstoke Road, near the quarry and walked down to the ground together. Ken Lane had been an R.A.F. pilot and was awarded the DFC, but would never tell the other chaps what he had done to deserve it.

For the rest of that season WOBs played their socks off and at one point had a real chance of topping the table for Somerset Senior League. As it was, they finished second, which was brilliant, of course, for a village team.

There was further excitement when one of the players, Roy Irwin, was spotted. A letter arrived from the official scout for Aldershot Town, inviting him for a trial. This letter must have made his day. Although I have no idea of the outcome, it must have meant a lot, as Roy still has the letter, which he allowed us to copy.

This epistle reflects the time. The paper is wafer thin and environmentally friendly, the ink comes from the nib of a fountain pen and there is a stylish flourish to the writing, especially the underlining.

While Worle Old Boys were entirely an amateur team, nationally times were beginning to change. The newspapers on

March 6th were full of the news of a transfer deal. Tommy Taylor, a 21 year old centre forward for Barnsley was bought by Manchester United for £29,999. He must have been a very happy and potentially rich young man. What a good thing that he could not foresee 6th February, 1958, when he would be one of the seven Busby Babes who lost their lives in the Munich air disaster.

Our local club were regularly allocated tickets for the F.A. Cup Final and ran a draw to decide who would go to Wembley. What a treat that was in 1953 – the year of the Matthews Final between Blackpool and Bolton Wanderers, which Blackpool and Stanley Matthews won 4-3. So, who travelled up to London on 2nd May to witness what was arguably the most exciting final ever – unless you supported Bolton? The lucky winners were R. Rodgers, W. Maggs, M. Herwig and R. Rowlands. Above is the cover of the programme they would have brought back as a souvenir. The tickets themselves were 3/6d, or 17p in new money!

Socially, Worle Old Boys never ceased to organise and fund raise. This year was busier than ever. They had already won a moral victory over the Church following the Comic Football row, but they also organised dances, described as Grand Balls, at the Church Hall. On Friday 12th June the Mercury published a photograph of the people of Worle dressed to the nines and attending the WOB dance. There was a live band, probably George Lock and his Orchestra, who played the hits of the day, a remarkable selection including Frankie Laine's 'I Believe', Lita Roza's 'How much is that Doggie in the Window' and the never to be forgotten 'Coronation Rag' by Winifred Atwell.

Everywhere you turned, the 'Green and Whites' popped up. They were outside Skidmore's in their numbers every other Saturday at about 1.30 pm to catch the coach to away games; they were training on the Recreation ground; they and their hundreds of supporters were rushing from pillar to post to back the four teams; they were on the carnival float in an odd variety of guises. Eric Maggs remembers no swearing on the pitch. Such behaviour meant an immediate sending off and, in any case, you couldn't aspire to be Stanley Matthews unless your manners were impeccable. Most of all they looked after their members and the families.

In December of 1953 they needed to do just that. On the 14th, there was a tragic accident near Annandale Avenue. A 22 year old cyclist, John Mayled, was fatally injured when he was in collision with a lorry. John had played for Worle Old Boys for many years and the club did its best to help his family. On Boxing Day, they played a testimonial match in his honour and donated the proceeds to his widowed mother and his sisters. This tribute appeared in the Worle Old Boys programme.

'As is already known, in a tragic road accident on 14th December, Johnnie Mayled, a well-known member of the Club was fatally injured in a road accident nearby. On behalf of the club we extend our deepest sympathy to the members of his family. Johnnie has played all his football with Worle and was a popular and enthusiastic player ... he was only too willing to play in any team and any position whenever chosen, which is the true mark of a good Club Man'.

51

Four members of Worle Old Boys Football Club, dressed for the comic
football match. John Mayled is on the right.

Habitually, at the end of a tiring, footballing sort of day players and
supporters gathered at H.Q., otherwise the Old King's Head in the
Scaurs to discuss matters and put the world to rights. Worle did
not, as far as anyone recalls, have any social workers then. Perhaps
we didn't need them.

The Cricket Club

What Eric Maggs is to football, Johnnie Tucker is to cricket. Thankfully, John has kept a lively archive of memorabilia relating to Worle Cricket Club, of which he became chairman on 28th May, 1953.

To put things into some sort of perspective, Brian Austin has traced references to Worle teams playing cricket as far back as the Worle Stars in 1870. Worle Cricket Club was established in March 1880 and continued until March 6th 1956. They built their own pavilion on the field behind Nut Tree Farm in the 1920s but, when normal service was resumed after the war, their home matches were played on the recreation ground.

In the year of our Lord 1953 the club was beginning to feel a financial pinch [there's nothing new under the sun] and this shows up from time to time in the club minutes. People with memories of the club have told me that the money trouble stemmed from a slight change of policy. Until the early fifties many of the local farmers and landowners had played regularly for W.C.C. but most of them, though well-heeled, were long in the tooth, so they lost more matches than they won. A decision was made to enlist some of the village's younger chaps, and the old farming fraternity found themselves watching glumly as the club became more and more victorious. Instead of backing the new lads to the hilt, the 'ancien regime' ceased to donate the previously generous prizes to the Christmas Draw. So the chickens, turkeys, boxes of vegetables and other tasty treats were no more, and people soon lost interest in buying draw tickets. This had been a major source of income and was sorely missed. Victory at the crease did not lead to financial stability so cuts had to be made and taxes levied, so to speak.

On January 22nd, a committee meeting, held as always at the New Inn, decided to increase subscription fees for playing members to £1. Saturday fixture fees were to be raised by 6d, and, in addition, a charge of 6d was to be levied for fixture cards. I can't help noticing that Wyn Charles, my uncle and a very good all round cricketer, proposed these increases. And he a good socialist boy.

Transport to matches was also a worry. The first suggestion, carried unanimously, was that any member who used their own car to take players to Saturday matches would be paid a suitable fee. Secondly, they decided to look into drive-hire costs. Wow.

The most far-reaching decision, however, was that *'in the light of present financial difficulties, Worle C.C. does not become affiliated to the County C.C. in 1953, with the proviso that the position come under review at a later date'.*

The first decision taken at the General Meeting that April [for all-comers, not just the committee] was very sad. They decided not to hold the Annual Club Dinner. Without the previous generosity of local farmers it was untenable. Cricket itself was also discussed. During the month of May they decided to have two practice nights to get back into form after the closed season. So Tuesdays and Fridays each week were booked on the Recreation Ground for practice, followed, no doubt, by a pint at the New Inn. After that, the meeting cheered up, and began to display its community spirit. Worle Old Boys Football Club were to be approached with a view to a cricket match in support of the Worle Coronation Fund, and in a further spurt of generosity, they decided to lend the club's trestle tables to Wick St. Lawrence's Coronation Committee for their children's Coronation tea party.

Several of the club's best players were from Wick St. Lawrence, including the Parsons boys, George Edwards and Ken Osmunds. Ken married the very fetching daughter of Cooks, the cider maker from Rolstone. Johnnie, relating this information, sounded somewhat envious of the combination of the lovely daughter and the cider. Another club member, Wilf Balaam, had strong associations with Wick – his mother lived opposite the memorial cross, by the Church. The club photograph was the last one known to be taken, late in 1952.

WORLE CRICKET CLUB - 1952

The new season opened optimistically, as reported by the Mercury, against Webbington, where the score card shows that Worle made 44 runs for 7 wickets [declared] to win the match. It is noticeable that several of Worle Old Boys players, notably Ken Lane DFC, and Ken Trego also belonged to the Cricket Club so that their entire year was taken up with one sport or the other.

The greatest drama of the season came after the last game had been played. There was unrest at the committee meeting on September 4th, a month after the Flower Show [this does become relevant]. The meeting was held in the New Inn and was to us, in the 21st century, jolly amusing. The game of cricket and the season that had just finished were not talked about. Tea utensils were first on the agenda. They had disappeared without trace from the pavilion on the day of the Flower Show, August 3rd. Good. There's nothing like a mystery.

On February 23rd, the Borough Council 'Parks, Parades and Sands' committee had given permission for the Horticultural Society to use Worle Rec. for their Annual Flower Show, with what was described as the 'usual facilities'. These facilities included the use of the pavilion – the one on the rec, not behind Nut Tree Farm. Someone evidently overstepped the mark and interpreted this as permission to make free with the Cricket Club tea things. Item 166 in the club minutes reads thus: '....that the secretary write a strong but tactful letter to the Flower Show Committee re the loss of the club's tea utensils on Flower Show day from the Pavilion.'

The shocking matter was not resolved until early in the New Year, when a list of missing crockery was submitted to Messrs Skidmore, and the estimate for replacement sent to the Flower Show Committee, who agreed to compensate the Cricket Club for its loss. Peace was restored, but there was a sorrowful end to the whole story. Three years later, on 7th February 1956 the decision was finally made to wind up the club and the crockery gets another mention '...that the crockery, mower and roller be sold and together with any cash balance outstanding be invested by G. Edwards and W. Parsons, who are to be trustees'.

It is a particularly sad thing when a village loses its Cricket team, but luckily in 1953 we did not see it coming and did not need to be comforted by the knowledge that it would rise like a phoenix from the ashes in the guise of Worle Century Cricket team, who regularly played in 20-Over evening matches thereafter.

One piece of memorabilia of cricket in 1953 may still exist somewhere. When I. Robins gave up as secretary early in the year something needed to be done to say thank you for his efforts. A bat was acquired and inscribed with the initials of all those who contributed to its purchase. This wonder was presented to Mr. Robins at the general meeting. How we would love to see it again.

It is worth mentioning that on August 19th England had regained the Ashes from Australia after 20 years. Four of the five test matches were drawn, so the country held its breath as the fifth test started at the Oval. This was the first time that Ashes Cricket was televised and there was great joy when Len Hutton led England to victory. For Wyn Charles there were memories rekindled of playing at The Oval for the RAF almost a decade before. Who would have believed that he would aspire to play for Worle C.C. on the rec?

Other Sporting Matters

There is, of course, sport and sport and I don't intend to attempt a definition. Perhaps darts should be described as a pastime, but however you view it, darts was big news in 1953.

There was a Worle Darts League which sported [sorry about that] sixteen teams of which five were based at the New Inn, Worle and two at the New Inn, Kewstoke. That must have caused some rivalry and confusion. The Lamb Inn, The Golden Lion and the Old King's Head all had teams and some teams travelled in from 'outside', namely the Woolpack, Boro Arms, Wick Wasps and the Aero Club. This Mercury report of 6th February provides the detail.

The New Inn, Worle, was definitely the Mecca for darts, even entering a team in the National Darts Championships. This must have been a complicated competition to organise, since the New Inn lost in the 4th round of the Somerset and Dorset division of 'The People' national darts championships to Salt House, Clevedon. 'The People' championships were first played in 1938 and eventually led to the setting up of the National Darts Association of Great Britain in 1954, so the New Inn was teetering on the brink of greatness.

The local pubs were proud of their darts teams and we have two posed photos of the players outside their spiritual homes,

smartly attired and well groomed. There is no date for this shot of the Old King's Head team, but it is included to demonstrate the serious nature of the activity and the fact that they won a cup, whenever it was.

Our four public houses also provided places for the men to take an interest in horse racing. Form could be studied and discussed and bets decided upon. Placing those bets was not a simple matter in those days. Betting shops were not legalised until 1st September, 1960, so bookmakers were a rarefied breed. Still, Charlie Perkins, a bookie from Weston was very helpful. He visited the Worle pubs on a regular basis, picking up the betting slips and the money. Some folk, including my grandfather, placed their bets at Skidmore's sweet shop, where a record of bets was put in the book 'out the back' and picked up later, probably also by Charlie. Now and then I was dispatched with a bob or two in my pocket to put a shilling each way on this or that horse.

Only rarely did these activities bear fruit. The Grand National was always a popular race for everyone to put a few pennies on. In 1953 Early Mist was starting at 20 to 1 and was fancied by Johnnie Tucker, who risked a bet on it. It came in first, of course, and John still lives in a bungalow named 'Early Mist' in honour of the horse. There is a picture of the profitable animal on Johnnie's study wall.

Many of the younger men who were involved in a range of sporting interests also met at the Century Club in Mendip Avenue. The original land for the Village Club was donated by Mr. Phippen, the builder, whose yard and shop were on the north side of the High Street, and the foundation stone was laid by Violet Lesley Hardwick in 1904. In the early years of the Village Club it was generally accepted that there was a no alcohol proviso in the deeds and this idea was strongly reinforced by a succession of vicars. This affected business adversely so that the club was eventually rescued in the early 60s by a consortium of young men who all put in cash to buy it. A look at the lease told them that the village had been duped, and the 'no alcohol' clause was a myth! From then on the newly Christened Century Club livened up.

Eric Vallance Cook spent his final evening as vicar of Worle in the Century Club with the members. In his farewell speech, he said, ruefully, that when he had arrived in the village in 1949 it was a lovely, quiet place, but he left it a gambling den. Game, set and match to the sportsmen of Worle.

The Schools and their people

Since the opening of the Secondary School in Spring Hill in 1940, Worle had boasted three schools, so, in theory children could be educated in the village from the age of four to fifteen.

Worle Infants' School

Situated in Mendip Avenue, the school was conveniently near Skid's sweet shop and was bordered by orchards on two sides. It was a solid little Victorian building which sat firmly on its foundations. At the centre of the school was the hall which was used for all activities that involved more than one class. Here, the piano was established to provide music for assembly each day and for nativity plays, singing lessons and all sorts. At the north side of the hall were: the cloakrooms with name pegs for each child; the head teacher's study, and a new facility for 1953, a school meals scullery approved by the Borough Council on the last day of 1952. This scullery provided running water, a hob to keep food hot and a serving area. The food was prepared and cooked elsewhere and delivered each day. I lived within fifty yards of the school so I never ate the school dinners and I haven't located anyone who did eat them, so no comment is possible.

The four classrooms opened off the sides of the hall, two on each side, although everyone I have spoken to only remembers three being in use. These rooms were furnished with bright Formica tables and little brown chairs, mostly arranged in groups to accommodate about 6 children. Youngsters started school when their parents and Miss Simcox, the head mistress, decided it was a good idea. This meant anything between three and five years old.

Miss Lewis taught the little ones in one of the west facing rooms. She was a gently spoken, sweet lady who tried her level bests to start everyone on the path to knowing their alphabet with the aid of flash cards: a for apple; b for bat......all with illustrations.

Mrs Hardboard, a comfortable middle-aged lady with motherly ways took the second year, but then it was necessary to steel yourself. Miss Simcocks, who taught the top class, was a tartar. She often used her study as a prison for naughty children, had a scratchy personality and gave out lines to be produced after school. Her favourite was: 'I must not talk in class'. This was open to interpretation, so it was possible to sit silently, not answering questions until she demanded to know why. Disciplinarian parents approved of Miss Simcox, easy-going ones found her hard work. My mother, a teacher herself, considered an assassination attempt.

Outside in the playground was the best tree in the world – our conker tree. In truth, it was huge – about four times as high as the school. The candle flowers in spring smelt glorious, the massive leaves could be peeled into fishbones and then the conkers arrived, millions of them. Every child took home hundreds every day at the peak of the season. Goodness knows where they kept them all. Nobody bothered about injuries, so as well as traditional games of conkers on string, the boys used them as projectiles in their mini-wars. Ron White was the only boy who could climb to the very top. What a hero.

There were very few toys to play with at break times, but the jungle-gym was popular for playing 'I'm the king of the castle' and there was a very mucky sand pit in one corner. The real down-side was the children's lavatories. Outdoors, and therefore wet underfoot as well as smelly, so that many children would go to great lengths to avoid using them, with dire consequences.

Worle Junior School

The Junior School was a Voluntary Controlled Church of England School perched at the top of Hill Road, next to St Martin's Church. This building had had an interesting life, starting as a tithe barn and later becoming an Elementary Church School, catering for local children between the ages of 5 and 14. The 1927 Kelly's Directory described it as follows: *'Public Elementary School [mixed] once a monastic barn, supposed to have been connected with the Priory of Woodspring but restored in 1866 and enlarged in 1911; the school will hold 258 children....'*

In 1953 Les Bull was the headmaster and he had another three teachers to assist him in his endeavours. The pupils were mainly drawn from Worle Infants' School but a small number arrived from Milton or St. Georges. There were about 35 in each of the four classes according to the school register records and, according to my memory, the furniture provided was as old fashioned as the building.

The desks were all arranged in pairs and most had benches attached. They were made of oak and had been engraved by several generations of the young of Worle. Every desk had an opening lid to allow for storing books and treasures, and a white porcelain inkwell in the right hand corner. The latter was very inconvenient for left-handed pupils, who consequently made more mess than anyone else. The ink monitor was expected to keep the inkwells topped up by pouring the smelly stuff from an enamel jug. Sitting on the desks resulted in inky circles on precious skirts or trousers. The wearing of school uniform was compulsory for special occasions, but generally rather lax. Some of the poorer pupils didn't possess a uniform and borrowed bits from here and there to appear in school photos or to go to Church services.

The school had a bank account, details of which are recorded in the Managers' Minutes. The opening balance on 1st January was £95/13/4d. Much of the income was derived from two sources; a bequest to schools from Stephens and Trapnells amounted to £42/15/2d and the headmaster paid a quarterly rent for the school house of £6/5/-. This latter was not generally known, the assumption being that the house 'came with the job.' By December 31st the balance had grown to over £150. There was little expenditure, the greatest item being the £10 expenses paid to S. Gibbins.

My contemporaries and I spent the first half of 1953 in the Infants' school with Miss Simcocks in charge of us, but on Monday 31st of August we 'went up' , in all senses of the phrase, to the Junior School and into the tender mercies of Miss Fountain, a white haired lady, nearing retirement and often away ill. We worked quite hard at reading and poetry, and I remember knitting in the afternoons. Interesting.

Mervyn Brown and Mrs Tripp completed the staff line up, but not for long. By the end of the year Terry Jones had been appointed to teach the second year, replacing Mervyn Brown.

Local attitudes to Mr Bull were diverse, depending, no doubt, on position in the community and general ability to be awed. He was a very tall, thin man with strong, pointed features, a yellow complexion and brillcreamed dark hair. I have talked to people who are still overwhelmed at the sound of his name and to others who considered him less than adequate. He was certainly a great patriot, spending whatever time could be justified on British History and on maps of the world which concentrated on the Empire – despite the fact that it was a Commonwealth by 1953. The Queen's Coronation oath made her Head of the

Commonwealth and Defender of the Faith, not an Empress, but this did not deter the headmaster.

Mr Bull also made it clear that he had favourites, and was particularly drawn towards the children of local landowners and businessmen. He was a very good shot with a board rubber, so I am told, though I don't remember witnessing this. The poor man would have much preferred not to have me in his class, partly because my mother was a teacher and knew all the same people as he did, and partly because I was inclined to question everything, which he hated.

Whatever else it was, Worle Junior School was a happy place to be. Everyone knew all of the other 120 or so pupils and probably their families and this gave the children a feeling of safety and stability. It was also very high on the list of successful local schools in terms of eleven plus passes.

In 1953 the 'Scholarship' exams, as they were often called, took place on February 3rd. Four members of the school's managers were co-opted to invigilate. It was a long old day for the pupils, who sat the first test, Arithmetic, from 9.30 a.m. to 10.45, with the Vicar in charge.

After break, [they actually called it Playtime] Mr Lutley oversaw proceedings for the General English test from 11.00 until 12.45. Then it was lunch, and

> Try this typical question from the arithmetic paper:
>
> A man left home at 11.30 a.m. and cycled 5 miles to a railway station at the rate of 12 miles an hour. He waited 10 minutes at the station and then travelled by train a distance of 36 miles at the rate of 24 miles an hour. At what time did he reach his destination?

those who had school dinners walked down to the Church Hall for nourishment, whilst the lucky ones went home for a rest. At five past two, it all started again with the dreaded Intelligence test with Mr. Tripp invigilating for 45 minutes, and finally a short burst of Comprehension for 25 minutes under the eye of S. Gibbins. This enigmatic 'S. Gibbins' was the school correspondent [secretary] and was never given a title in the minutes, so could have been either gender.

The pupils, and their anxious parents, had to wait for months to find out how well they had done. Eventually results were sent to the headteacher and letters to the parents of successful pupils. No letter, no luck. Often children were relieved not to pass, preferring to go to the Secondary School in Spring Hill, which was familiar territory, than to the unknown reaches of the Grammar School, miles away by the No. 40 bus on the other side of Weston.

The 'lucky' ones still had to suffer some more. Examination success was only the first stage, now there were interviews. This process was used across England and Wales. Children who were near the top of the results table were given a short interview, five minutes or so. These took place at the Grammar School, where the pupils were faced by the Headmaster or Headmistress [depending!] and two school managers, usually men. The poor little mites who were further down the list were awarded long interviews. This must have been harrowing and those who suffered it said that there was more written work to be done during this time as well as the interview.

The interview process whittled out a few more pupils who were not invited to attend one of the two Grammar Schools. So the 35 children in the top class at Worle Junior School landed up in a variety of places. Most went to Worle Secondary [for boys and girls], some to the Girls' or the Boys' Grammar Schools and a few girls opted for Winterstoke Secondary [no boys allowed!] This effectively broke the children up into separate camps each of which had names for the other. Grammar School pupils called the Worle children 'Worle Worms' and they called us 'Grammar Grubs'. Everyone thought their own school was the best, so there was no real discontent.

With the serious business of selection behind them the school turned its attention to other matters. The Coronation dominated the curriculum for the early part of the year. The decision was made to celebrate and educate by producing a Royal Heritage Pageant. This extravaganza was to begin with the Romans and end with the final appearance –Charles Dickens. The village, and indeed the town, contributed generously. Mr Chaplin gave the

use of his field behind the school on the north side of Church Road without charge; Mr and Mrs Stephens allowed the children to use their home, 'Hillside', as a dressing room; Messrs Stone and Cox provided the amplification; scores of people supplied fabric for the costumes, and the whole thing was topped off by an array of wigs loaned by Lloyd and Osborne in the Boulevard.

The weather was kind and Chaplin's field had never been so colourful or as busy as it was on the evening of May 21st. The people of Worle, suitably attired in hats and gloves, necessary in the presence of royalty, turned out in

huge numbers and happily paid their 6d for a programme. The children who took part still recall the day happily. The names of the main characters were proudly listed in the programme. Henry VIII was depicted by John Middleton and Elizabeth the first was Marion Jones.

Mr Bull was thrilled with the whole thing and managed to get permission from the council to put on edited highlights in Grove Park later in the Summer. This was not such a happy occasion –it pelted with rain and actors and spectators were drenched and miserable. Still, one out of two wasn't bad.

The school had a Parent-Teachers Association whose primary function was to raise funds to help the school and the village. In 1953, of course, they wanted to do their bit for the Coronation Fund. On March 14th they held a 'Coronation Grand Whist Drive' to raise money. The entry fee was 2/6d, which seems exorbitant for the time but the prizes were generous - £5 for the highest score amounted to a week's wages. The Cricket Club's idea of a match against the Old Boys may or may not have come about, but certainly the PTA organised a comic cricket match. The men borrowed their wives' clothes to dress up in and the women wore their husbands' cricket whites. The photograph reveals the interesting fact that Vallance Cook played in this match, dressed as a woman. Obviously his objections to the Old Boys game had been forgiven and forgotten.

With the fund-raising, pageant, and the Coronation in the past, the school went on a trip to Stratford-upon-Avon. I say 'the school' but it may have been just the older children. The group certainly made an impression on an American tourist, who photographed the children and sent a print to the school, dated and with a note.

Mr Bull's classroom

Above: The Parent Teacher Association dressed for cricket
Below: The pupils in Stratford

Worle Secondary School

The official opening of the school took place on April 2nd 1940, a Tuesday. The date had been planned for the 1st, but it was thought an inauspicious idea to open on April Fool's Day. In 1980 a book was published to mark the 40th anniversary of Worle School and I heartily recommend this wonderful little tome. It describes the building in Spring Hill as 'A Modern School on a Green Hillside', and reminds us that there were mixed feelings locally about its 'low built, glass-sided classrooms, divided with lawns and surrounded by open, draughty corridors.'

Thirteen years later, in 1953, the school was a well established and well loved part of the community. Pupils started at the age of 11 and most left at 15 years old, at the end of their 4th year, although it was possible for pupils who wanted to attempt O Levels to stay for an extra year, and some did. There are many photographs of groups of 15 year olds, about to leave and set out on life's adventures. These children in class IVB may have come from the parishes of Milton, Kewstoke, Hewish or Wick St. Lawrence, but most were from Worle.

By 1953 the school, in common with all other schools in the area, had dealt with evacuees, rationing, air-raids and staff who were up all night on fire-watching duties. After all that Mr Bisgrove, the head teacher,

71

must have been very happy to deal with austerity and education. However, there were other problems to deal with, not least over-crowding. Marion Matthews remembers [on page 16 of the 1940 to 1980 book] that the staff rooms and Hall were used as classrooms, and the Hall had to be cleared to put up the trestle tables for school dinners, which were eaten in two sittings.

Photo taken late 1940s or early 1950s
front: Mr Matthews, Miss Snellgrove, Mr Prosser, Mr Bisgrove, Miss Baker, Mr Finney, Miss Rossiter
Back: Not known, Mr Stephens, Not known, Mr Atkinson, Not known, Mr Holly, Not known

Despite these difficulties, staff and pupils flung themselves into the annual production with vigour. 1953 was to be the year of 'Little Red Riding Hood' and a look at the report in the Mercury gives us an idea of just how much work was involved. Everything needed for the performances was produced in the school; sets, costumes, lighting, the lot. The acting, singing and dancing were all highly praised and on five consecutive evenings in February the pantomime played to packed houses.

The Mayor, who would remain in office until May, was Alderman R. W. Brown and he attended a special extra performance with his wife. At the end of the evening, the head girl of the school, Pamela Watt, presented him with a cheque for £100 to be used for the East Coast Flood Relief Fund. This picture from the environment Agency gives us a flavour of the time and helps us to understand why, for once, the Coronation Fund took second place. Only ten days previously, 307 people had died in what is still described as the worst national peace time disaster to hit the United Kingdom. The storm surge in the North Sea, combined with low atmospheric pressure had resulted in floods which shocked the nation. The Netherlands came off worse still, with over 1000 deaths. No wonder the children and staff decided that the money should go to help out.

Pupils from the early 50s remember a much stricter regime than today. 'Standing on the Line' was a much dreaded punishment. The line was outside Mr. Bisgrove's office and badly behaved pupils were told to stand there until they were given permission to return to class. This meant that the whole school knew who had been in trouble and the embarrassment was excruciating. Achievements and misdemeanours reflected on your house which was another worry. The houses were named for local ranges of hills: Mendip, Quantock, Brendon and Blackdown and there was fierce competition between them. Quantock often won at Sports Day. Successes were celebrated on Prize Giving day from 1952 onwards and the first Senior Party was held even earlier in

December 1948, but they were subdued affairs, held in the afternoon. Evening parties didn't begin until 1959.

Most of the school's team sports and athletics took place on the Recreation Ground, so an ex pupil told me, but the gymnasium was an asset and was great for netball practice. Perhaps that is why the whole school netball team was chosen to represent the County.

Finally, Marion Matthews described Friday morning assembly when this prayer was always spoken aloud by the whole school:

Remember, Lord God, for good,
All those brought up here who have gone out into the world. Keep in their hearts the lessons learned here: of Truth and
Honour, Fair Play and Generosity;   And
grant that no misdeed of theirs, or evil word, may sully the
good name of this school;
And that, faithfully serving God and man, they may repay their
nurture.   Amen

Carnival Time

This was, to a seven year old girl, one of the best days of each and every year right though childhood, but 1953 was the best of all. All the children adored the carnival and none of us had the least idea how much work and trouble it must have been to organise it. Reflecting upon the effort required from the vantage point of the aching bones of late middle age it becomes obvious that some serious planning and dedication was required.

The first mistake is to assume that Whitsun Monday just meant the carnival. Carnival day was much more than that! Wait and see.

World War II had caused such frivolities as this to be put on hold, but the good old British Legion worked hard in the early fifties to restart a much missed institution and by 1953 it was a full blown bonanza.

Early in the year, if not before, the plans were laid for entries. Some were serious tableaux, beautifully presented, and vying for the Grand Challenge Cup. These took months of work, but don't imagine flashing lights and the huge floats of Weston's Winter Carnival. This was Worle. They used tractors, ancient flat-bed lorries and anything they could get their hands on. The walking classes were popular and arranged in age groups to encourage the young. One year, possibly 1952, I found myself being dressed in the black attire of an old lady, whilst Eric Priddey was poured into an old gent's trousers and jacket. Our faces were lined with eyebrow pencil and we were informed by Mrs. Priddey [who was very bossy] that we were entering as Derby and Joan. I complained, but to no avail, and we won the class.

Best of all were the comic groups, walking and on wheels. It must be admitted that the more serious entries featured the ladies of the village, whilst the entertaining ones were put on by the men. The pubs competed against each other to get the loudest cheers in the hope of winning the Skidmore Challenge Cup, which Skidmores often won themselves.

They had to get on with things well in advance, so that the programmes could be designed and printed to be sold at 4d each.

Many villages chose a May Queen each year and Worle's May Queen was also Carnival Queen. Shirley Lickes was chosen for Coronation Year. She had two fetching attendants, Margaret Ackland and Margaret Burgess, and was crowned at the Church Hall by the vicar's wife. There was no parading in swimsuits, I'm glad to report. The decision was made at a Saturday dance in the Church Hall – it may have been the Football Club dance. In the midst of the dancing, the young men were encouraged by the Master of Ceremonies to take to the floor with the young village maidens and the Queen and attendants were chosen from the dancers. Nobody is very clear about who actually chose them – perhaps the chairman of the British Legion, R.C. Cousins was a judge, maybe the president of the football club, R.W. Thomas was co-opted. I dare say the vicar had his say. Whoever it was, they chose Shirley who lived in Greenwood Road and her picture appeared in the Mercury, of course.

Pat Slade, Nee Tabrett, who was Queen in 1956 remembers being taken, with her attendants, to Trevors' dress shop, the poshest in Town, to be kitted out for the big day. Mrs Trevitt, who ran a hotel on the sea front with her husband, Councillor/Captain Trevitt, bought the dresses every year, and the year that Pat was Queen, she also invited Pat and her parents to dinner at the hotel and treated them like royalty.

On 25th May, 1953, the three young women – Shirley and the two Margarets - were joined on the float by four little girls, one on each corner. The float was all red, white and blue flowers and the girls had red, white and blue striped ribbons in their hair. Irene Kingsbury, Ann Wyatt, Diane Jeeps and Raye Jones [me] played at princesses for the day. I look somewhat droopy in the photo, having suffered from *excitement tummy ache* all night.

The floats and walkers gathered after lunch in Kewstoke Road near the quarry entrance and facing towards Kewstoke, which was odd, since everything had to turn in the quarry entrance to head back towards the village. This had to be achieved by 2.45 p.m. when the British Legion Silver Band struck up their first number and led the parade off around an excited and expectant village. Behind them walked the children's fancy dress classes, walking; then the prams, push chairs and various decorated cycles and, at last, the first float, the Queen and her maids of honour.

The adult walkers and floats came after the Queen, which was just as well, since many of these entries involved buckets of water, men in grass skirts and other varieties of drag. The most eye and ear catching entry was the exploding car, featured in a Mercury picture, and put in by Skidmore's, of course. Sadly the picture is too poor to reproduce here.

Naturally, the Coronation had to be featured. The Carnival was, after all, only a week before this great national occasion, so we enjoyed Worle's effort at producing a golden coach, horses – well one pony and one donkey - and a very young monarch.

This lovely old snap against the background of 'North Worle' makes quite a statement

about the nature of the changes the last 50 years have brought. Newton's Lane wanders down the hill on the opposite side of the road, and the house with the distinctive chimney is still there. Go and see.

Finally, the rear of the parade was brought up by St. John Ambulance, proud in their uniforms.

The route went south along Kewstoke Road, it passed the Old Forge and Gunnings Stores, turned right along Church Road and down Coronation Road. At the corner of Greenwood Road, the youngest children, all in fancy dress, waited to join the procession. The High Street was packed; people crammed the pavements and sat on garden walls; my grandparents waved a union flag as we went by. At last Station Road was reached and we trundled happily down to the recreation ground.

Well, that got the day started, but there was much more yet. The rec was crammed with stalls, there was a huge marquee, where tea was served, a skittle alley where a pig could be won and an area chalked out ready for sports. Nobody thought that winning a live pig might be a nuisance. A bit of space could always be found for a good porker and a local butcher would oblige when the time came.

At 3.45 p.m. the winners of each category in the parade were presented with prizes by a succession of local dignitaries, including Mrs. Trevitt.

Formalities over, the Comic Football Match, obviously much loved locally, since there had been one only three weeks previously, kicked off. Ladies were playing, so it only lasted 30 minutes. I dare say this was to protect the dear little flowers. The tea tent became the focus of attention and the Silver Band that had led the parade played gently until the sports began.

There were sixteen races, ranging from under 5s to veterans, with variations including potato race, three-legged race, slow cycle 'race' and wheelbarrows. Some actually took it seriously, including my mum, who won the ladies' 100 yards, as usual.

The desire for fun remained unsated, and the swingboats and roundabout did a roaring trade. Finally, at 8.00 pm precisely, George Lock and his Dance Orchestra struck up, and the marquee was full of pretty girls and lusty young farmers. The Carnival Queen opened the dancing and four and a half hours later, exhausted by the whole day, she had the last waltz with the man of her choice.

R.C. Cousins, chairman of the British Legion organizing committee and his huge band of helpers had played a blinder. As Enid Blyton used to say, 'they all went home tired, but happy'.

The Coronation, and all that

The crowning of Queen Elizabeth II was a huge international, as well as national, event. Dignitaries and Royalty the world over travelled to London to witness the occasion. The lives of the ordinary people of Great Britain had been taken over by the preparations for June 2nd since the funeral of the Queen's father, George VI. Remembering this time, the Telegraph newspaper published an article on the first day of the new millennium. It reads as follows:

'In 1953, Britain seemed to be on the brink. But the brink of what? Romantics hoped that the Coronation would usher in an era of serenity and progress. The radiance of the young Queen and her charming little family would revive a country that was weary, over-regulated and under-nourished. The sovereign's youth, supported by the maturity of the Prime Minister, Sir Winston Churchill, would magically release Britain's ingenuity and flair.'

I have to say that, as a child of the time, I was never aware of the adults in my world – and there were lot of them - being weary, and I certainly wasn't. Maybe the over-regulation refers to rationing, which may have been a worry to the women, but was also a challenge, and didn't bother the children at all. We were not under nourished in Worle. So there.

Like the rest of the country, the village was looking forward with some vigour to the BIG DAY. There was a feeling of a new Elizabethan Age on the horizon. The knighting of Churchill in the Queen's birthday honours list was universally popular, and if some thought it should have happened sooner, it was a very suitable way to say 'thank you' to Winnie in the run up to the Coronation.

Almost everyone in Worle had some hand in the fun-raising and preparations. The schools flung themselves into it, of course, but so did other children's organisations. Sunday schools, Guides and Brownies, Youth Clubs all raised money. Bob a Job week was brought forward to contribute. The sports clubs, the two

churches, everyone did something. Quite a few locals took themselves off to London to be a very wet part of history, sleeping on the pavements under mackintoshes and umbrellas and only able to get a glimpse of the young Queen by using the cardboard periscopes on sale everywhere.

The fund raising had resulted in £250 to be spent on 'A Good Day'. The Mercury report tells us that Mrs Trevitt was as generous as she had been to the Carnival Queen, this time providing cakes sufficient to feed the whole village!

Although Worle traditionally celebrated on the recreation ground, on this occasion Tripp's field was the venue – good idea, since it made the day extra special and brought the main focus of the fun into the heart of the village. Before the day, good old Mr. Tripp moved the animals and the marquees were erected, the fun fair put up and 500 trifles were made for the children. These last were red, white and blue and frankly, not great.

WORLE REACHED ITS TARGET

Worle's target of £250 for Coronation celebrations was attained. So, also, was the ambition to have "a good day." Everyone joined in the revelries on Tripp's field.

Over 100 older residents were at the Church Hall for TV, refreshments being provided. A large iced Coronation cake given by Mrs. Trevitt, wife of Cllr. J. L. Trevitt, was cut. Mrs. Trevitt gave another beautifully decorated cake for the children's tea, at which there were 500. Each had a trifle, coloured red, white and blue, and was presented with a souvenir spoons.

"Go As You Please"

Sports for young and old were held and there was a "Go as you please" concert, interrupted for the relay of the Queen's speech. Dancing and "the fun of the fair" went on until a late hour.

Most of the streets were decorated with bunting but The Maltings was by far the best effort and was still being featured in newspaper articles in 1984. There is a photograph of the householders taken on Coronation Day somewhere, but I have failed to locate one clear enough to reproduce here. Prizes were awarded to households that made a special effort to deck their dwellings with red, white and blue. One prize winner was the cottage at 95 Church Road, pictured below, with the proud owners.

The Church Hall was called into use for about a hundred of the village elders to join 20 million other viewers watching the ceremony on television. Others had invested in a TV set of their own and invited neighbours and friends around to watch. At 2.00 pm the televisions were switched off and everyone made their way to the field. It was packed with stalls. The sports started at 2 o'clock and continued until 4.30 when the children were fed in the marquee – 500 of us were given spoons and mugs as souvenirs. I have lost mine.

The community singing was great fun – all the songs of the day were attempted, some with more success than others. The ones that stand out in my memory were 'How Much is that Doggie in the Window? And 'Maybe its Because I'm a Londoner'. Such moments stay in the memory and are very good for patriotism and community spirit. What we didn't know was that, almost simultaneously a young man, name of Elvis Presley, popped into a recording studio in Memphis, Tennessee, and asked if he could cut a demonstration disc.

Dancing in the marquee began at 8.00 p.m. and went on until 1.00 in the morning. This time the dance was free of charge, and the Carnival Queen, bless her, attended again in full regalia.

Everyone I have spoken to remembers what they were doing on June 2nd 1953. The Golden Lion provided a refuge for some of the men, who watched on the pub TV away from their sentimental women folk, and with a pint in their hands. This was an interesting reflection of a national controversy which had been much talked about. Televising the ceremony on the BBC was not a foregone conclusion. There was considerable feeling, especially in the Church and the government. Churchill told the young Queen that her advisors and the cabinet did NOT feel that she should be subjected to a live television broadcast of the ceremony in Westminster Abbey. The Queen told Churchill, politely, that she was being crowned, not the cabinet, and broadcast to the people it would be.

The Church's concern was not for the stress the Queen would be put under, but for the very idea of a religious ceremony of that importance being watched in public houses by people enjoying a pint. The Queen's intervention ensured that that was just what occurred. If the day did nothing else, it put television at the heart of the British nation and brought the name Richard Dimbleby to everyone's lips.

The Daily Round

We have to remember that 1953 was an exceptional year, but the most important thing was that the heart of the village continued to beat at its normal rate. The things that are small if regarded from the bigger picture become all important to individuals and families. None of us would have survived comfortably without our shops and, what I believe we should call, retail outlets!

Not all the shops were in the High Street: others were dotted about to pick up the business of those who found it more convenient not to walk too far. Mrs Jones kept a small grocers shop half way up Coronation Road. This little corner store is happily remembered by Sue Ryall who worked there as a young woman, and the following is in Sue's words:

'Apart from bottles and tins, most goods were sold loose. The only things frozen were ice creams and that was mainly a summer item. There were no frozen vegetables so things like potatoes, veg, dried fruit and bacon were weighed or cut as needed.

The bacon came in as half a pig wrapped in a muslin cloth which Mrs. Jones washed and kept for cleaning the windows. I soon learnt to bone and divide the pig into the various cuts, long back, short back, gammon and streaky. We sliced the bacon on a hand slicer into the thickness the customer wanted.....The bacon pieces were kept in a large old fashioned fridge and every so often we had a clear out and all the old bits of bacon joints were taken out into the back garden and burnt on a bonfire. The garden had a lovely smell of smoked bacon for days afterwards.'

Sue's evocative description of this and other matters is typical of the affection with which people recall day to day village life.

Kewstoke Road, and the immediate area, which had been the centre of Worle in earlier times, still hung on to a few shops, of which Gunning's Stores was the most notable. Owned and run by Henry T. Gunning, the store had been established in 1700 and was the oldest established in the district. Early pictures show it as Spinner's Supply Stores, a grocer and provision merchant. In Kelly's directory of the mid 50s, Gunning's was one of the few businesses to have a telephone number – Weston 3010. Roy Gunning and Margaret Gunning, Henry's children, continued to run the business until its closure.

Further along Kewstoke Road, still on the west side was Moody's Stores, often known locally as 'Thacker's', because C. Thacker ran it. How Gunning's and Moody's both survived on local business heaven knows, but they did and even the existence of Thyers at Glebe Nurseries, almost opposite Moody's, didn't put anyone out of business. Thyer's business was mostly a plant nursery, but also sold some produce from their market garden which stretched along Kewstoke Road from the top of Hollow Lane to Somerset House,

And so to the High Street, the best street in the whole wide world as far as I was concerned. It had everything anyone could ask for. Starting at the Weston end, we first came to Staples Dairies, which operated out of Manor House Farm [Tel Weston

3098]. There was an interesting sounding household at Manor House Farm, listed in Kelly's as Morgan Glyndwr, Jones, Jn. and Staples, S. P. H.

Marshall's the newsagent was on the corner of High Street and Annandale Avenue and mainly did papers, tobacco and sweets; then came Ivy Lodge Guest House and Cafe, open all year, and run by Mr and Mrs Searle. Mrs Tripp, wife of Alfred Tripp, sold the milk from the farm in a shop at the front of the farm house if you could get her to hear.

And then there was Vowles and Sons, bakers and confectioners that stood at the corner of Greenwood Road. The bakery smelt delicious. Every Saturday morning I was sent out shopping and always bought doughnuts which were a special treat for after lunch on Saturdays. These were not doughnuts as we know them now. They were the long ones, but were filled with artificial cream and jam, which was universally loved. Bread was coming off the ration in 1953 and a small loaf of white bread could be bought for sixpence-farthing. How good is that?

Most of the rest of the shops were on the south side of the road, with the exception of Phippen's funny little shop which sold bits and pieces for DIY and building. Mr Phippen's family had built many of the houses in the High Street at the turn of the century and he was still active in the industry in the 50s.

The other bakery in Worle was Neathway's. In a double fronted house set back a little from the road and with a central path up to the front door, Mrs Neathway presided over the baking and selling of bread. In order to purchase the loaves, you had to walk up the lane at the side of the house and enter through the back door, where the smell of baking overwhelmed the customer. Looking back, it seems that none of Worle's bread had to move more than half a mile before it was on the table being buttered with local butter from the dairies.

Edwards, the butchers, famed for its faggots, was next to the bakery.

My childhood home was on the south side in the middle of a row of shops which started with Central Stores, the residence and business of George Priddey. George and his wife Sue lived mainly above the shop, with just a kitchen and store room behind the shop downstairs. It also had the biggest fridge in the world. No-one had fridges then, so this was quite a phenomenon with two doors and provision for hanging meat. George had a rather unctuous manner and ran around the shop gathering anything his customers requested and bringing them back to the counter. Sue Priddey never, never worked in the shop, although sometimes she would stand in a corner, watching what was going on. Even if George was run off his feet, Sue never shifted. He was tall and thin, Sue was short and fat and I always thought of them as Jack Sprat and his wife.

The village chemist shop was Bessell and Raikes, between Priddey's and my house, so I'm an expert! This shop provided all our family toiletries and quite a lot of the presents purchased for the women of the family.   There was an electric clock in the window which could be relied upon to be accurate, unless there was a power cut. 'Go and look at the chemist's clock' was a regular shout from the adults in our house. The pavement narrowed at this point to allow for the little front gardens of two villas still used as dwellings, but after that there was quite a stretch of shops.

The Bristol Co-operative Society occupied the first two. One was their butchers shop and had a marble counter, sawdust on the floor and a cheerful chap, often with plasters on his fingers, who served. The Co-op grocers, next door again, was a wonder. The counters at either side were served by staff who all had their regular stations. As with all shops at the time, the goods were brought to the counter and the bill was 'totted up'. The money and the bill were put into a little brass pot, which was screwed into the overhead wire contraption, the lever was pulled and the pot went on its short journey to the cash desk. This was housed in a wooden structure, like a secular pulpit. Here sat Margaret with her till and her knitting. When a pot of money arrived overhead, she put known her needles, unscrewed the pot, took it down, opened the till, put the change in the pot and sent it on a return trip to the counter! There were four or five wires leading to different areas of the counters and nobody seemed to think it was at all odd.

Three ways of getting along the High Street

Beyond the Co-op was Weaden's Cycle shop, where my first and only bike was purchased, second hand. Besides bikes, there was a small selection of boys' toys of which the favourites were the models cars, displayed in glass cases. It was also possible to purchase a selection of batteries to fit the torches and bicycle lamps on display.

Every child in the village loved 'Skids' – not necessarily the ironmongery, but the sweet shop. The jars were right in front of you as you went through the door. Lemon, pink, green, mauve, red, orange, white and black treats were stuffed into each jar and you could smell the sugar from outside. At the very end of the long, thin shop was the freezer where skid's homemade icecream was stored. This marvellous stuff spoiled you for any other icecream for life. Even elderly ladies [by which I mean my grandmother] who swore by a brick of Wall's between two wafers, had to admit that Skid's was best.

Mr Dunning ruled over the Post Office, a remarkably dark, dusty shop which seemed, because of the poor lighting, to go back for miles. It sold a strange array of drapery and most of the children in the village were brought up in Post Office socks. The business end, so to speak, was right by the door on the left. Mr Dunning was the only person I ever saw behind the dark wooden counter, so I assume he must have felt that he was living his life in gaol, as there was a forbidding metal grill to protect the money from being stolen. Poor Mr Dunning had a pipe inserted through a hole into his neck. I suppose he needed it to breathe, but this time I didn't ask.

Wet fish was available every day fresh from the marble slab in Porters. Norman and Grace Porter also sold a good variety of vegetables, mostly grown in their own ground. They kept a small field right opposite the shop and Norman could be seen there digging and harvesting, happily. He was a tallish, very chatty man and Grace was small of stature but very well covered and with a quite amazing bosom. I have heard it said that you could lay a table for eight on Grace Porter's chest. Grace also had red hair, which was not natural, so she must have used henna, and she wore bright red lipstick in a massive lover's bow. It was an interesting overall picture, but in all other respects Grace was perfectly normal.

I was very fond of 'The Tiny Shop', which was just as it sounds. The left hand wall was lined with shelves full of wool, patterns were displayed in books on the counter and there was a selection of toys, this time for girls, and of a handicraft nature.

Powell's shop was described as a fruiterers, and marked the end of the 'Parade', as it was called. There were a few more establishments further along, including Dawson's, which was another grocery shop and Prewett's the newsagents.

At the far end, at the 'Terminus', was the Imperial Laundry, owned by the Wigg family and run by Patrick Wigg. It undertook laundry, dying and cleaning and employed many of the village women. Picking up the laundry was an experience. The steam and the noise were both penetrating, so that if you had to wait any length of time you came out again exhausted and dripping wet, It was, I think, true to say that the women who worked there were mostly of an impressive size with strong, red arms from the heat, which is remarkable. You would think they would have sweated it all off.

Fussell's Rubber Company employed scores of the men. The new, prestigious offices in Station Road could not be started until 1954, because of the building restrictions still in place post-war, but the plans had existed for some time and the offices were officially opened in 1955 by Sir Ian Orr-Ewing, who expressed a wish that his own facilities in London could approach the same standard. Claude Champion, who took over as Managing Director in 1945 carried on the company's traditions of quality service and social conscience. 'No passengers here' became a company motto. Fussell's supplied Rubstuds, Silent Knight heels and the rest of their range countrywide and, remarkably, were featured in a six page article in the 'British Shoeman' magazine.

There was, you may have noticed, not an estate agent in sight. Masters was the first to arrive a little later, taking over the co-op butchers, and nowhere near as useful, as we all used to eat meat and nobody moved.

The women shopped daily and used the opportunity to swap gossip, but Saturday morning was so busy, you would have thought it was Piccadilly Circus. People bustled about using the road as well as the pavements to rush around, but at lunch time, then as now, it suddenly went quiet until Monday and the usual bustle began again.

Almost all families ate around the table together daily, but the atmosphere varied from house to house. Some families were noisy, chatty and full of laughter, discussing everything under the sun, with political matters at the top of the list and local chit-chat also on the agenda. In other households I had the opportunity to visit, there was silence whilst eating, and especially if the news was on the wireless. Luckily for me, my home was one of the noisy, chatty ones. Table cloths were ubiquitous and varied, with white linen or cotton being the most popular for meals and some new fabric called seersucker becoming fashionable.

Funnily enough, 'fashionable' was not a fashionable word in the 50s, but remarks like 'there's lovely things in the shops' were frequently on the lips of women who had been deprived of anything lovely for over a decade. Suddenly, it was possible to buy brand new fabrics to make dresses and skirts, but not in Worle. For this kind of purchase a trip into town was called for. Hats and gloves were donned and the ladies waited for the 40 'bus at the 'bus stop outside the Co-op. The chatter was gentle, never shrill and Christian names were seldom used. 'Good afternoon, Mrs This,' or 'How are you, Mrs That?' and other polite exchanges took place between women who had known one another for donkey years.

The women also knitted the woollens for the entire family, so the two spinster sisters who kept The Tiny Shop did a roaring trade. Knitting women had one or two interesting habits, the most irritating of which was the inability to answer a simple question. 'What time are we going out, Mum?' would be inexplicably answered by 'thirty-three, thirty-four, thirty-five...' It only became clear how important it was to count stitches when the whole class started mumbling numbers under their breath in Miss Fountain's knitting lessons at the Junior School.

Weddings 50s Style

The Mercury in 1953 did not use anything like as many photographs as they do today. Wedding pictures were practically non-existent, but there were a few reports of nuptials and several folk have rummaged through family albums to provide us with clues about the fashions of the day and how we went about organising a wedding.

Despite the inclement weather that winter of 52-53, Wyn Charles and June Wetten happily planned their wedding for Friday 20th February: the first of the year for which we have pictures. June was a Bath girl – by which I mean that her family came from Bath, not that she spent all her time luxuriating. She taught at Banwell School – her first job after College – and shared a tiny flat with her friend, Jean, just off the Boulevard. Wyn Charles also worked at Banwell School and they soon began a romance. Wyn lived in Worle High Street with his parents, sister, brother-in-law and niece, and was well known to the sporting fraternity, who called him Chas, as one of Worle Cricket Club's stars. June and Wyn announced their engagement at Christmas time and the families began a frantic six weeks of organising the day. No one seemed to take two years to plan a wedding in 1953.

This wedding was at the church of St. Thomas a Becket in Bath, with a reception nearby, so Wyn and his family had to travel to the far reaches of the county for the ceremony!

There were two little bridesmaids attired in soft red velvet with dutch caps. June carried white flowers and wore a lovely 50s gown with tiny satin buttons and a stand up collar.

The photograph below shows, from left to right:
Rachel May Charles, Mervyn Jones, Norman Charles, Wyn Charles,
June Charles [nee Wetten] Mr and Mrs Wetten and in front, the
two bridesmaids, Elizabeth Crabbe and Raye Jones, [me].

I had to promise not to smile too broadly, as my two front
teeth had fallen out and I was in trouble for fiddling with them too
much.

Wyn and June were married for almost 54 years and had
two sons and two grandchildren. Wyn was a navigator in the RAF,
then a teacher and finally a writer. June became a teacher in
Mendip Green School and still lives in Church Road.

*****

On July 19th Charles Bennett, 29, a clerk from Stanley Grove married Brenda Grove, who lived with her parents at 28 Church Road. There is a short report in the Mercury, so we know that the three bridesmaids wore lavender taffeta. I do hope it was sunny. They lived near enough to the Church to walk along for the ceremony, which is so romantic.

On August 22nd, Ray Ackland travelled from Worle, where he had been born in New Cottage, The Scaurs, to St. Saviour's Church and there he married his girl, June. We have pictures thanks to one of our members, my friend Mary Pinn, who phoned June at her home in Lanarkshire and asked her to send photos. After many happy years of married life, Ray passed away and June moved to be near her son in Scotland. She loves it there and is being sent one of our calendars for Christmas by another member, Ray Palmer. June Ackland's dress is very similar in style to June Charles's, tiny buttons up the front and a collar.

Of all the possible days in 1953 to choose to marry, the trendy thing to do was to pick September 12th. Why? Because that was the day that Jack Kennedy married Jacqueline Bouvier and Camelot was reborn. The young JFK was a junior Senator at the time of his marriage and Jacky was reporter for the Washington Times Herald. They met in 1951 and two years later Jacky found herself in London covering the Coronation for the paper. Maybe the enforced separation cleared Jack's mind, but whatever the reason, JFK proposed as soon as she returned and they were wed in Newport, Rhode Island on September 12th. The photograph suggests that it was a lovely wedding, but, say what you will, she bought the wrong dress – no buttons up the front, no collar.   What was she thinking of? Jack looks distinctly doubtful.

Never mind, back in Worle, on the same day, Shirley Vaughan from Greenwood Road, got it right.   Dear little silk buttons, stylish stand-up collar, St Martin's for the ceremony, Church Hall for the reception and her mum did all the catering, including the cake.

Maurice Bryant, Shirley's new husband, looks chuffed to bits; her two sisters were bridesmaids, and Jenny, the little one in the photo tells in her memoirs of the new fridge the family bought to keep the food fresh. Hurrah.

Bessie Coles lived at 1 Kirklands, High Street, with her Auntie, Mrs Peglar, her uncle and her cousin, Carol. She was courted by John Beakes, a fitter, four years her senior, who lived at Preston House, Lawrence Road and on August 1st, they married.

Bessie's dress was made for her by a friend who had worked for Hardy Amies and, of course, it had the collar that was such a symbol of the times, but the buttons were down the back and on the sleeves and the waist was 23 inches. Carol Peglar, the older bridesmaid wore a turquoise dress and the little one wore pink. Bessie still has the dress and a little box with fragments of the fabric and ribbons to remind her of the day.

One last marriage for a special mention is Joyce Edwards to Jim House. These two both belonged to Young Farmers and it was a popular match. Worle Cricket Club's minutes record a decision to spend a guinea on a gift for the couple, which considering WCC's straightened circumstances was very generous. Joyce appears in some of the Cricket Club photos, so must have been a supporter and tea maker extraordinaire.

Y.F.C. MEMBERS WED AT WORLE

Two members of Weston-super-Mare, Banwell and District Young Farmers' Club, Miss Joyce Edwards, twin daughter of Mr. and Mrs. P. G. Edwards, Laurel Farm, Worle, and Mr. Jim House, only son of Mr. and Mrs. H. G. House, Barton Farm, Winscombe, were married at St. Martin's Church, Worle, by the Rev. E. Vallance Cook.

The bride, given away by her father, wore ivory brocade, with orange blossom headdress, and carried red carnations. She was attended by the Misses Jean Edwards (twin sister), Jane Frost and Pam House (bridegroom's cousins), and Mary Puddy (friend), who wore lilac tulle over taffeta. Mr. Richard House was best man, and Messrs. Michael Frost, Michael Collings, Lewis and Dennis Edwards were groomsmen.

A reception was held at Bird's Hotel, Winscombe, after which the couple left for a honeymoon in Scotland, the bride travelling in a beaver-lamb coat, with mustard accessories.

Other Weddings at St Martin's that year

February 14^{th:} Alfred John Wilmot, 23, butcher of Cumberland House, High Street married Ann Pearl Bellin, 21, a shop assistant.

February 21st : Preston William Downing, 36, a motor engineer of Avonia, High Street married Elsie Winifred Browning, 27 of 49 Hill Road.

February 28th : Dennis Arthur Urch, 23, Bricklayer, of 10 Kewstoke Road, married Nancy Trego, 20 a Hair dresser from 9 The Rows.

March 16th : Howell Joshua Davies, 52, a widower married Frances Victoria Porter, 50, widow from Hampden Road.

Here there is a long gap, three months, in fact. It is said that Vallance Cook would not conduct wedding ceremonies during Lent, but Easter was in early April, so Lent began in mid February. This suggests that there is little truth in the story.

June 8th: Geoffrey Howard Mason, 24 a stock manager married Milly Edwards of The Laurels, High Street.

July 18th: Valentine Beacham, 28, married Margaret Knight,21, of 1 Preanes Green.

July 25th: Geoffrey Hawkins, 22, a mechanic married Margaret Venning, 20, a cashier of 1 Bolton Terrace.

September 21st: Albert Henry Borwick, 25, a market gardener married Margaret Lilia Diamond, 22. Both lived at The Nurseries, Kewstoke Road. Wow.

December 19th: A Christmas wedding for Derek Matthews, 19 years old and Jeanne J'Anson, 20 years of The Garth, Worle.

Each of these marriages has its own story, of love, misery, happiness, children, all lived in quiet privacy, except for one. Camelot can never be private. Poor old Kennedys.

Baby Boomers: The Tail End

The post year boom in new babies was mercifully beginning to slow down by 1953. Couples who had been forced to put family life on hold for the duration of the war had had seven years to catch up but there were still more new babies than normal.

Expectant mothers [definitely not 'pregnant women', please] made some choices about where their children were born. Many chose home births with a midwife in charge; many chose Ashcombe House and Sister Bidmead and the unlucky few had to settle for the maternity ward at the General Hospital. Caesarean sections were a rarity. Mothers who opted for Ashcombe House could expect to stay there for ten days, during which time they were treated as invalids and kept to their beds for at least four or five days. Babies lived in the nursery, not next to the beds, and were given their night feeds by the staff. Mothers lay in bed happily chatting, knitting and reading. Babies were presented to them, clean and tidy, to be fed and then taken away to do any crying at the other end of the building. Breakfast, lunch and dinner were brought in on trays; flowers, cards and chocolates arrived with the visitors. This taste of the high life must have been an extended holiday for hard pressed women. **No** wonder it was catching on.

The shock of returning home to a demanding family was profound. Washing, ironing, shopping, cooking, cleaning, knitting, sewing and all the rest of it recommenced, and there was a new baby to 'see to'

The well off had Silver Cross prams with springs and big, smooth wheels. The quality of the child's bedding was inspected by all the other women in the village whilst the children were left outside shops, unattended. The thought of anyone wishing to steal an extra baby would have raised a smile – who would be that crazy? Most mothers used hand-me-down prams or settled for less opulent down-market models. At home, the very young were kept in cages, otherwise known as play pens, and justified, I'm sure, as a safety precaution. Once children could walk they were often taken out on reins or in small, fragile looking pushchairs, very different from the plush vehicles of the 21st century.

Carry cots were popular in the 50s for lugging the infants around, but only with families who had a car, and these were few and far between.

Some of the fruits of the women's labour are recorded in the baptismal records of St. Martin's Church. We don't know how old these children were when they were Christened, but it does give some sort of record of the times.

February 15th: Linda Christine Bull, 18 Hill Road, daughter of Ronald [aircraft fitter] and Christine

Peter David Snelgrove, Coronation Road, son of Percival [cook] and June

March 1st: Georgina Florence Gardner, Ebdon Road, daughter of Frank [engineer] and Rosa

Jeffrey Phillip George, Myrtle Villa, Coronation Road, son of Edward [driver] and Sarah

April 12th: Marion Elizabeth Neathway, 'Tresco' Bristol Road, Worle, daughter of Ronald [baker] and Rose

Stephen Paul Williams, 27 Hill Road, son of Edward [carpenter] and Evelyn

May 24th: Mary Lilian Crease, Lawson Villa, Coronation Road, daughter of Ken [market gardener] and Esme

June 6th: Verity Ann Disney, Summer Lane, daughter of Oswald [master builder] and Eileen

Philip Jeffrey Ham, 'Woodlands' High Street, son of Geoffrey [lorry driver] and Joyce

June 21st: Janet Mary Rodger, 20 The Rows, daughter of James [bus driver] and Doris

July 12th: Joanna Roseff, Spring Hill

July 12th: Alison Rennie, Spring Hill, daughter of David [Air Ministry] and Monica

August 2nd: Avril Jane Richards, Greenwood Road, daughter of Frank and Clarice. Known as Jane, this girl was in my class at school and had had her 7th birthday on March 3rd the same year. This reminds us that some of these baptisms were not small babies.

August 9th: Pauline Elizabeth Disney, 43 Milton Green, daughter of John [fitter] and Jean

October 4th: Carolyn Mary Deal, 'Hillside' [The house behind the Junior School, where they changed for the pageant], daughter of Edward and Elizabeth

David Nicholas Petty, 85 Church Road.

October 20th: Pamela Jane Lucas, White House Farm, daughter of Brian [dairyman] and Jean.

In Memoriam

There are disruptions to be dealt with by each and every generation and the post war period was no exception. Firstly, the village had to say a final goodbye to a smattering of its residents. The sad, premature death of John Mayled was perhaps the most difficult to come to terms with, but there were others.

Reports in the Mercury mention four other deaths in 1953.

Mrs. L. E. Phillips, born Lillian Lewis, was a member of the Salvation Army and was a Weston girl.   Her father had been a dairyman in Orchard Street, Weston, but she lived her last years at least at 2 High Street, Worle. Her husband had run a butchers shop in town until his retirement and was also a Salvationist. Latterly she had attended Milton Baptist Church but Lillian's death in January was followed by a funeral at the Salvation Army Citadel in Carlton Street, attended by scores of family and friends.

The next reported death was that of Jack Hadley. Jack's full name was Ivan John Hadley and he was a member of the Royal Antediluvian Order of Buffalos.   An extract from their official website reads:

> *In so far as surviving records can prove, the earliest known traceable date of a Lodge of the Royal Antediluvian Order of Buffaloes is 1822 at the Harp Tavern, Great Russell Street near Drury Lane Theatre and was created by stage hands and theatre technicians who had been denied a long held privilege extended to them by the actors and artists of the day.*

I had no idea of the origins of this club, which I gather is rather like the Masons.   What a variety of people we had in the

village. Anyway, Jack Hadley's funeral in June 1953 was very
different from Lillian Phillip's. At Jack's farewell, no women were
mentioned for a start.

The report reads as follows: *Mr Hadley served in the Royal
Navy for 28 years and saw active service in the two World Wars.
Latterly he was employed by the G.P.O. as a member of the delivery
staff.*

*Principal mourners were Messrs. I.W.F. Hadley [son]; W. Hadley and
T. Hadley [brothers]; M. Pople [son-in-law]; F. Trego [brother-in-
law]; F. Hadley, C. Trego and H. Trego [nephews]*

*Also present were Messrs C. F. Townsend [Asst Postmaster,
representing Head Postmaster]; F.G.C. Harding [Inspector]; R. A.
Thorn {Asst Inspector]; J. B. Gilbert [Rep. Union of Post Office
Workers] and a large number of Postmen. Retired Officers of the
G.P.O. present were H. F. Mason [Inspector]; W.E. House [Asst
Inspector]; R. H. G. Tubbs [Asst Inspector]; L. J. Curry, [Head
Postman]; A. H. Thomas, E. S. R. Banwell and A. E. V. Mann.*

The funeral was conducted by Vallance Cook, but the
report does not say where Jack was buried. It mentions a son, but
does not say anything about Jack's wife, who survived him. His
son-in-law attended the funeral, but it doesn't mention a daughter.
The conclusion has to be that this family decided that the funeral
should be men only – not entirely unknown at the time. Often the
women stayed at home and said a quiet prayer, whilst the men
went to the service and the graveside.

WAS WELL-KNOWN WORLE FARMER

DEATH OF MR. H. G. CHURCH

Mr. Herbert George Church (57), who farmed at Grape Vine Farm, St. Georges, Worle, died at the home of his sister, Miss Elsie Church, 14 Greenwood-road, and was buried at Worle Cemetery on Monday.

Mr. Church, who was born at Grape Vine Farm, and who took over the running of the farm from his father, retired about four years ago owing to ill-health.

During the war he assisted with the billeting of evacuees, and was also a member of the Banwell section of the Special Constabulary. Among those present at the funeral was Mr. C. J. Cook, who was the Banwell "Specials'" section commander.

A service at St. Martin's Church, Worle, was conducted by the Rev. Shirley-Price.

Mourners : Messrs. C. H. and W. E. Church (brothers), H. G. Wallis (nephew), G. and A. Marshall, E. Weare, W. A. Walter, also representing Messrs. H. H. and S. A. Walter (cousins).

Also present : Mrs. M. Champion, Mrs. E. Nuttycombe, Mr. and Mrs. H. C. Plaister, Rev. G. R. Osborne, Messrs. C. J. Cook, B. A. Osmond, F. H. Plaister, W. A. Cox, J. Steer.

Floral tributes : Elsie; Charlie and Maud; Will and Edie; Bert and Kathleen; Annie and the Wear brothers; Annie and George; Herbert, Stanley and Wallie; Nervy and Stan; Clifford, Rene and Brian; Mrs. S. A. Hall and friends of the Woolpack; Frank, Amy and Marg.; Mr. and Mrs. Cumine, Gillian and Roger; Mr. and Mrs. W. Hall, Vera, Doris and Donald; and Mr. and Mrs. Burraston; Peter Chaplin and family; Mr. and Mrs. M. R. Champion, Ivor, Rita and Maureen; Mr. and Mrs. F. Plaister

In August a report appeared of the death of a 'Well Known Worle Farmer'. He was Mr. H. G. Church of Grape Vine Farm. This time the report is much more relaxed and intimate in its tone. There is a family feeling to it, and women attended, which is reassuring. Mr Church died at his sister Elsie's home at 14 Greenwood Road but it omits to say that poor Elsie had died in April, aged 68. Even so, there is an atmosphere of loving care surrounding his death.

We can see from the report that Herbert – I wonder what his friends called him – was 57 when he died and is buried in the Churchyard, but the service was conducted by Rev. Shirley-Price, not Vallance Cook. I wonder why. Perhaps the vicar was on holiday.

Many of the mourners' names are familiar, but I couldn't help noticing that one of the floral tributes came from 'Nervy and Stan' – an unusual name, Nervy.

In October, another local character, Flo Kingsbury, nee Fletcher, died. She hadn't been right for some months, and her death had been expected. Florence Emily Kingsbury was the matriarch of a very big family, all of whom were in the Church for her funeral service, or sent flowers.

I particularly looked to see if her grandchildren went to the funeral, but I see that they stayed at home and probably joined the family later for the wake.

Flo's granddaughter, Irene Kingsbury, told me that Mrs. Cann was her Aunty Barb; Jack Fletcher was Flo's brother and lived in Coronation Road; Mrs J. Dunston was Flo's sister and known as Aunty Polly – incidentally, Aunty Polly was Lilly Blizzard's mother; Bill Fletcher, Flo's brother, lived the in 'Windy Ridge', High Street. This was one of the new houses on the Weston side of Annandale. Irene also remembered that earlier that year she and Jenny Vaughan pushed Irene's brother in a pushchair up to Lyefield Farm to visit Flo. They took bacon sandwiches and a drink and came away with a memory to treasure for life.

During March, the deaths of Stalin and Queen Mary also occurred. Queen Mary's death made the Mercury, but Stalin's did not. However, the death of the Russian leader had a far greater international impact. Winston Churchill and President Truman

FUNERAL OF WORLE FARMER'S WIFE

MRS. FLORENCE EMILY KINGSBURY

The funeral took place at St. Martin's Church, Worle, on Tuesday, of Mrs. Florence Emily Kingsbury (68), Lyefield Farm, Worle, who was the wife of Mr. A. J. Kingsbury, a farmer and dairyman at Lyefield Farm for 36 years. Mrs. Kingsbury had been in ill-health for some months.

The funeral was conducted by the Vicar, Rev. E. Vallance Cook; and mourners were: Mr. A. J. Kingsbury (husband); Mr. and Mrs. W. Kingsbury, Mr. and Mrs. F. Kingsbury (sons and daughters-in-law); Mr. and Mrs. L. Cann (son-in-law, not daughter); Mr. and Mrs. J. Fletcher, Mr. and Mrs. W. Fletcher (brothers and sisters-in-law); Mr. and Mrs. J. Dunston (brother-in-law and sister); Mr. and Mrs. G. Cox (brother-in-law and sister-in-law); Mr. John Phillips (uncle); Mr. and Mrs. C. Griffin, Miss Joyce Oliver (friends).

Wreaths

In loving memory from her devoted husband and family; All her grandchildren; Polly, George and children; Brother Jack and sister-in-law Irene; Will, Edie and Pat; Edie and Jack (Milton); Hett, George; Nina and Laurie; Harry, Vi, Bill and children (Bristol); Annie, Charlie, Ella and Brian; Bill, Olive and Geoffrey; Alice and Ted's family; Auntie Rose, Lil and Charlie; Lanie, Kate and Martha; Flora and Bill (Northam); Lil and William Jones (Guildford); Alice and Albert Kingdom (Porthcawl); Lena (Uley); C. Hurst; Mr. and Mrs. Cunningham; Mr. G. Cann, Joan and Fred; Gret, George and Sandra; Jack, Kate, John and Alan; Don and Brenda; Mr. and Mrs. P. Bartlett; Frank, Amy and Laelia Chapman; Lonie and George Searle (Oldmixon); Joyce; Percy Palmer; Aunt Jess and Uncle Jim (Burnham); C. and M. Webber.

Undertakers: H. Pitman and Son.

109

made statements couched in diplomatic language. A national
newspaper said:

*'..he will be remembered for instigating political purges in which
tens of thousands were killed. He was also behind the introduction
of farming collectives which led to a famine and the death of 10
million people. His death is expected to provoke a power struggle
within the ruling Politburo.*

In 1953 the village also said farewell to other old friends. Funeral
services and burials took place for:

18th March: Margaret Amy Jewsbury, Sunnyside, Locking Rd East,
Worle, aged 83.

13th February: Robert William Henry Tucker, 2 Station Road, Worle,
aged 77.

10th March: Harry James Flock, Cave View, Worle, 78.

2nd April: Frank Syms, 'St Helens', New Bristol Road, 47.

8th April: Eliza Church, 14 Greenwood Road, aged 68

1st May: Jams Block, 'Green Park', New Bristol Road, 80.

29th May: Edward John Crocker, Bridge Farm, Worle, 79

24th June: Albert Henry Heard, 21 Church Road, aged 67

3rd July: Alice Elizabeth House, Town House, Worle, 76

29th July: Harold Arthur Herring, 1 Parkstone Villas, Greenwood
Road, aged 58

28th September: Edmund John Phillips, 4 Preanes Green, 34

10th Oct: William Robert Anderson, Greenwood Road, 72

10th December: Oliver Tucker, Ebdon Road, aged 51

28th December: Christopher Radford, 7 Bolton Terrace, Coronation Road, aged 75.

All lives lived in Worle, in the shadow of the Church that oversaw their goodbyes, and all, we hope, still remembered.

Less Serious Matters

Although the roads were as quiet in 1953 as they would be at five in the morning now, people still managed to bump into each other and digress in small ways. Motoring accidents were still sufficiently novel for the Mercury to think it worthwhile to report on the smallest incidents. Oddly, July seems to have been a dangerous time: three different incidents were reported.

When Arthur Eames, a sixty-five year old gentleman of Old Bristol Road was involved in a minor accident at the junction of Bristol Road and Manor Road, the Mercury put in a few lines. Mr. Eames had sustained a shoulder injury and was treated at Weston Hospital.

Shockingly at the time, Sandra Gill, a seven year old girl who lived in Spring Hill was admitted to Weston Hospital to be treated for cuts and bruises. She had been hit by a motor bike ridden by Kenneth Vincent from Milton Brow. The whole class at school was horrified and Sandra was a heroine.

Finally, Brian Disney, then a rash twelve year old who lived in one of the Council Houses in Kewstoke Road, fell from his bike and was rushed to hospital with a fractured skull. Although I tend to dislike the Health and Safety culture we live in, I must admit that Brian would have come out of his fall better if he had worn a helmet.

A court case in October ended in two motorcyclists from Bristol being fined £5 each for driving in a manner dangerous to the public. An innocent Worle man, Norman Stanley Huish, a farmer, of Brooklyn, Lawrence Road, was driving southward down Station Road. He turned right into New Bristol Road and signalled his intention to turn right into a garage. His van was struck by a motorbike ridden by Mr. Broadhurst, who was flung from his machine. Another motorcyclist, Mr. Lacey was also injured. Police Constable A.J. Smith interviewed Broadhurst and Lacey, the defendants. Graham George, Cheltenham House gave corroborative evidence and Arthur William, 5 Castle Acre, New Bristol Road appeared as a witness.

I have no memory of PC Smith, but PC Bird, who was our local police constable for many years, had his own moment of glory when he caught the unfortunate Reginald Hussey riding his bike without lights in Worle High Street. Reginald was not a Worle man, he lived at 7, Council Houses, Wick St. Lawrence and had to appear at Petty Sessions to be fined five shillings for his 'crime'.

Criminal Tendencies

This riding without lights incident, brings us on neatly to other issues connected with unlawful doings, and there are amazingly few reports of crime in Worle within the pages of the local paper.

A long, detailed and somewhat tedious report of Fraud appears in the paper on February 27th. To paraphrase, a chap named Lount seems to have gone about extracting money under false pretences rather successfully for a while, until, presumably one of his victims had had enough and the whole sorry tale became public knowledge. This 'public knowledge' was often, in those days a worse punishment than anything the law could inflict. One of Lount's victims was John Sprackman who ran Coronation Garage. Lount hired a car from John the previous October – fancy that, car hire in 1953 – and although he paid up in dribs and drabs he kept extending the hire period and gradually fell further and further behind with payments. Previously, Lount had extracted cash and cheques from several trusting souls including one William Cole Glukes, a shop manager in Totterdown Road, who was taken for a long and expensive ride and who told the bench he had trusted Lount implicitly. He parted with hundreds of pounds to enable Lount to purchase calculating machines which could be sold at an impressive profit. The machines were never purchased and the money was never seen again.

It is such a sad tale of woe. You can imagine Lount, needing cash and convincing himself and everyone else that he was on the edge of a successful deal. He probably looked successful by the standards of the time, turning up to extract cash driving a newish car, which he had hired from the unsuspecting John Sprackman. Oh dear.

Some folk were definitely struggling for ready cash and had to resort to borrowing from acquaintances. My parents were always a soft touch and were caught out twice, though I shall mention no names. One chap who had lived in Worle for a while and knew my parents, turned up at the house one day as if this was a normal occurrence. He drank tea and chatted, much to the bemusement of my family and finally asked if they could spare £4 to get him 'out of a hole'. My daft Dad parted with his hard earned pennies and Chappy disappeared, never to be seen again. Well, only once. In Woolworth's one day my Mother started behaving oddly. She dived behind a pillar. When I questioned her she explained that Mr. So and So was close by and she didn't want to meet him because HE owed HER money. I found this hilarious, and it still makes me laugh out loud. They didn't learn from this, and later parted with £20 [you could have bought a second-hand car for that with no trouble] in response to a plea from a friend. It turned out that another of our relations was similarly duped and no one recovered the cash. C'est la vie.

Towards the end of June the word 'vice' was mentioned in connection with a criminal charge brought against a Worle man. I advise you not to become too excited about this vice, which was one 'borrowed' from the RAF camp and screwed to a bench in Moor Lane to assist with building works in progress. Hopes of a red light district must be dashed. Charles George Nutt lived at Willow Mead, Moor Lane and worked as a cleaner at Locking Camp. An Air Ministry 'chain pipe vice' took his eye and he 'borrowed' it to assist with his life's work of constructing a bungalow.

When Detective Constable Wade turned up at the bungalow he found the vice, attached to a bench. Nutt swore he intended to return it and the Bench, by which I mean the magistrates, gave him the benefit of the doubt. The case was dismissed, but I do wonder if Mr. Nutt kept his job at the camp.

And that is the end of reported crime in Worle for 1953. I have no doubt that much more went on beneath the surface, but people dealt with matters differently then. One incident resulted in a small fracas behind the beer tent at the flower show, and was never brought to public notice. One task that PC Bird had to carry out on an annual basis was the delivery of a notice around the local farms, telling the farmers that the sheep had to be dipped forthwith. This entailed a rather social walk or pedal around the village, sampling a cider at each stop. Cheers.

Compared with crime in the country as a whole, this was tame stuff, for 1953 was the year when 10 Rillington Place and the name John Christie were splashed across the papers. Fifty years later the Telegraph recalled, in a retrospective article, the effect that this heinous crime had on the country.

'Here, the threat seemed to be moral. The notorious 10 Rillington Place murders, in a slum called Notting Hill, presented an England that was anything but Merrie. Three years earlier, a man called Timothy Evans had been hanged for killing his wife and infant daughter at the house.

Now more bodies were found in a cupboard. John Christie, a former occupant who had given evidence against Evans, was found to have committed at least eight murders on the premises. He confessed to killing Mrs Evans, which meant her husband had been wrongfully hanged.

It was a stark reminder that mistakes in administering the death penalty are permanent, as was the Derek Bentley case. Bentley was a hooligan with a low mental age who was hanged in 1953 because his younger accomplice in a robbery shot and killed a policeman. Bentley was under arrest at the time. Nonetheless, he was hanged.

The cases set in motion the campaigns that would eventually end the death penalty in Britain.

The Flower Show

Worle Horticultural Society was central to the heart beat of the village. Ruled by the seasons and peopled by local landowners, this happy band grew vegetables, fruit and flowers in gardens, market gardens, orchards and fields.

Mostly this was a business carried out to make a living, but my goodness, there was pride involved and the time to show off was August Bank Holiday Monday [the first Monday in August in those days] and the place was Worle Recreation Ground, in the main marquee, where the judging for Worle Flower Show took place. People from all over the County put entries in the show in classes which included: Amateurs, Open, Market Gardeners, Homecrafts and Domestic Science. It was an enormous and prestigious show, renowned in the world of horticulture and warranted a whole page of the old, massive Mercury.

There were 768 entries for the 1953 Flower show, which was held on August 3rd. These entries were vying for the honour of carrying off one of the eleven cups on offer, including the new Skidmores Cup for the highest aggregate of points in the home crafts and domestic science section, which Mrs. H. J. Burrows won.

For some years, gladioli had pride of place, but this year the prettier, softer, aromatic Sweet Pea was re-established as Worle's favourite flower and better still, Mr. E. Dowling, a 'weekend gardener' from Compton Bishop was triumphant. He was a miner who spent his working days hewing coal below ground, so his win was very popular.

Best in Show was S.C. Love of Yatton with an outstanding collection of vegetables – potatoes, tomatoes, peas, carrots, leeks, cauliflowers and celery.   Mr Love also carried off the Royal Horticultural Society's medal for most prise money in the amateur and open sections. Local name mentioned in dispatches were C.H. Fry, Mrs. E. J. Blake and Mrs. E. Thomas, who were brother and sisters.   Mrs Blake and Mrs Thomas were champion flower

arrangers and, I'm proud to say, decorated the Chapel for my wedding.

This photograph, given by Janet Bartlett, was taken at the 1958 show, but gives the uninitiated an idea of the grandeur of the occasion. Notice, too, that the gladioli are back in force.

Although the marquee and its treasures were the main attraction at the Flower Show, there were other considerations. The Horticultural Society always invited a 'star' to open the show. This year the Mercury published a photograph, almost impossible to see now, with the caption *'Worle Show – Miss Dawn White, the variety star, who opened Worle Show, is here admiring some of the exhibits accompanied by members of the Committee.'*

So who was she? Well she appeared at the Hackney Empire and the Alhambra, Bradford as 'Dawn White and her Glamazons' in a turn called the 'Golden Age of Music Hall'. The Alhambra describes Dawn and her ladies as 'big, enormous, colossal'. They were second on the bill to Frankie Vaughan, my idol as a girl, so they must have been OK. And, of course, dear old Bruce Forsyth was bringing up the rear. Anyone who saw her opening the Flower Show had touched greatness.

Outside the marquee, the usual attractions were available: sports, skittling for a pig, swing boats and stalls where the prize was a poor little gold fish in a jar. The ladies inhabited the pavilion, where tea and cakes were consumed in large quantities. This, if you remember, is the site of the disappearing tea things and caused the Cricket Club to demand recompense.

It is amazing how often we were all willing to put up huge tents, organise on a great scale, sit on committees, run the hundred yards, dress up in drag, make fancy goods for stalls, and dance. Whatever profession you followed, wherever you lived, however overstretched or comfortably off you were, you were part of this thing that was Worle. You cared for the young, revered the old, gossiped about everything, knew what everyone was up to and enjoyed it all. How lucky we were.

****

Diary of a Year in our Lives

January

Thursday 1st: There is no bank holiday today.
The New Year 's Day holiday will not begin until 1974.
Worle Junior School's opening financial balance is £95/13/4d.
Sir Ian Orr-Ewing, Weston's MP, is knighted in the New Year's honours list.
Permission is given by the council for a new scullery to be provided at Worle Infants' School. See Council minutes.

Friday 2nd: Notice in the Mercury of a Ratepayers' Association AGM to b e held on 28th January.
First Worle Guide Company meeting at the Vicarage, Church Road in the outbuilding at the back, this and every Friday at 6.00 p.m.

Saturday 3rd: Worle Old Boys 4 Totterdown Athletic 2
Papers report that East Coast floods have resulted in over 300 fatalities.

Sunday 4th: Worle Methodist Chapel, Lawrence Road services at 11 a.m. and 6.30 p.m.
St. Martin's services: 8.00 a.m. Holy Communion; 10.00 a.m. Holy Communion; 6.00 p.m. Evensong.

Monday 5th: Weston Borough Council Housing Committee agree to spend £10 each on the 'aged persons dwellings' at The Rows

Tuesday 6th: Worle Brownie Pack met at the Church Hall at 6.00 p.m. and on subsequent Tuesdays. Nora Jefferies is Brown Owl.

Wednesday 7th: Women's Fellowship meeting at 2.30 p.m. in the Methodist School Room, Lawrence Road

Thursday 8th: Half day closing for village shops.
Bell ringing practice at St. Martins.

Friday 9th: Council meeting report in Mercury: Green Belt may not be in Development Plan
Mercury report on WOB game played on 3rd January.
Guides 6.00 p.m.

Saturday 10th: Worle Old Boys at home to Shepton Mallet. WOB 6 Shepton 2. See programme

Sunday 11th: Worle Methodist services 11.00 and 6.30; St Martin's 8.00, 10.00 and 6.00

Monday 12th:

Tuesday 13th: Brownies. Nora's log book tells us we played Ships and Boats

Wednesday 14th: Women's Fellowship

Thursday 15th: Half day closing. Bell ringing practice.

Friday 16th: WOB football report in Mercury 'Worle Returns to Form'. House robbery reported in Old Bristol Road
Guides 6.00 p.m.

Saturday 17th: WOB Grand Dance at the Church Hall. Dancing from 7.30 until 11.30. Ted Coles Band. Entry 2/- .

To Whom it may Concern notice, dated today, and appearing in next Friday's Mercury, states that Maurice Wells, Solfereno House, Lawrence Road will no longer be responsible for his wife's debts.

Sunday 18th: Usual Services at St. Martin's Church and Worle Methodist Chapel.
Burial at St Martin's of Margaret Amy Jewsbury, 83 years

Monday 19th:

Tuesday 20th: Brownies.
Eisenhower installed as US President. His picture was all over the front page of the Daily Mirror.

Wednesday 21st: Women's Fellowship. Lawrence Road

Thursday 22nd: Worle Cricket Club meeting at New Inn. See minutes   Worle Junior School Managers' meeting. See minutes book   Bell ringing and choir practice

Friday 23rd: Mercury report of a chimney fire at 7 Preanes Green. Fire Brigade called.
Mercury report of death of Lillian Phillips, 2 High Street
WOB 10, Williton 3
Guides

Saturday 24th: WOB away to Wells City Reserves, see programme
Wedding of Ivan Walter and Valerie Harrington

Sunday 25th: St. Martin's services, 8.00, 10.00 and 6.00
Methodist services 11.00 and 6.30

Monday 26th:

Tuesday 27th: Council Estates and Plans committee give permission for a pair of semis to the built in Madam Lane

Wednesday 28th: Ratepayers Association AGM. 2915 paid up members.

Thursday 29th: Half day closing, Bell ringing and choir practice

Friday 30th: Mercury report WOBs 6, Taunton British Railways 2.
Sir Ian Orr-Ewing spoke in Commons on the Sunday Observance Bill.

Saturday 31st: WOBs away to Wells City.

February

Sunday 1st: Methodist Services: 11.00 and 6.30; St Martin's at 8.00, 10.00 and 6.00

Monday 2nd: Worle Junior School bank account records the receipt of £6/5/- in respect of rent of the School House from Mr. Bull, the headmaster.

Tuesday 3rd: Scholarship [11+] examination day. Invigilators: Vallance Cook, Mr. Lutley, Mr Tripp and S. Gibbins.
Brownies

Wednesday 4th: Borough Council received letter of complaint from Ratepayers Association about poor snow clearance.

Thursday 5th: The end of sugar rationing and its half day closing, but Skids stayed open.

Friday 6th: Mercury Darts Report. Darts matches played today at the New Inn, the Lamb, Old King's Head and Borough Arms
Wells City 3, WOBs 1

Saturday 7th: WOBs Reserves away to Knighton in Suburban League game. Pick up the coach at Skids at 1.30 p.m.

Sunday 8th: Worle Methodist services 11.00 and 6.30; St Martin's 8.00, 10.00 [including baptism of Susan Ethel West] and 6.00

Monday 9th: Council Business meeting at Church Hall, 7.3-. Serving councillors for Milton and Worle Ward: H. S. Allen; F. C. Bessell and J. L. Trevitt all present to give information and answer questions.   Little Red Riding Hood, Senior School Pantomime, first night in the school hall, Spring Hill

Tuesday 10th: Little Red Riding Hood, Spring Hill.
Brownies, Church Hall. Pat Fuzzard, Carol Peglar and Valerie Edwards enrolled at this meeting.

Wednesday 11th: Little Red Ring Hood, Spring Hill
Women's Fellowship, Lawrence Road.

Thursday 12th: Half day closing.   Little Red Riding Hood, Senior
School.   Bell ringing and choir practice.

Friday 13th: Schools break up for half term
Guides cancelled for last night of pantomime.
Orr-Ewing spoke in the Commons on Criminal Justice Bill
Burial of Mr. Tucker, who lived in Station Road.

Saturday 14th: Valentines Day Wedding of Alfred Wilmot, of
'Cumberland' High Street to Anne Bellin.
WOBs away to Odd Town

Sunday 15th: Usual Church and Chapel services

Monday 16th:

Tuesday 17th: Brownies

Wednesday 18th: Methodist Women's Fellowship

Thursday 19th: Half Day closing
Schools In-service training day

Friday 20th: Schools still on in-service training, except Wyn Charles
[High Street] and June Wetten both teachers at Banwell School,
who married today at the bride's Church in Bath. Betty Jones, the
groom's sister skived the in-service training at Hutton school, too.
Full report of Senior School Panto in Mercury, including cast
Odd Town 1, WOBs 2 – Mercury report

Saturday 21st: WOBs at home to Ilminster Town;
Worle Reserves visit Banwell. The coach leaves Skids at 3.00 p.m.,
so it must be a late kick-off
Wedding of Preston Downing and Else Browning

Sunday 22nd: Worle Methodist services 11.00 and 6.30
St. Martin's at 8.00; 10.00 and 6.00. Baptisms at 10.00 service of 4
children of the Cox family from Hertfordshire.

Monday 23rd: Parks, Parades and Sands committee of Borough
Council granted 'usual facilities' at Worle recreation ground for the
Flower Show on August 3rd. Iron and Steel Nationalisation Bill
voting in Commons. Aye 250, Noes 205. My father, triumphant,
rubbed his hands together and announced this with delight.

Tuesday 24th: Shrove Tuesday. Pancakes
Estates and Plans committee approved alterations to the cottage at
42 Church Road, a house and garage to be built in Hawthorn Hill, a
bungalow to the built in New Bristol Road, bungalows in Spring Hill.
They refused permission for a hoarding at Westonia Cottage.
'Thinking Day' programme at Brownies. Magic Carpet to fly round
world.

Wednesday 25th: First day of Lent. Vallance Cook was strict about
this and sometimes refused to marry people during this 40 days in
the wilderness. He must have 'relented' this year since Dennis and
Nancy Urch married on the 28th.

Thursday 26th: Half day closing, bell ringing and choir practice

Friday 27th: Fraud case reported in Mercury. Mr Lount was a con-
artist who cheated many people, including John Sprackman at
Coronation Garage.

Saturday 28th: Darts Individual Knock-Out Cup at Old King's Head.
Dennis Urch married Nancy Trego at St. Martin's, lent or no lent.

March

Sunday 1st: St David's Day. Usual services at the Churches, but St. Martin's included the baptisms of Georgina Florence Gardner and Jeffrey Phillip George.

Monday 2nd: Council declare Rock Cottage, Lawrence Road, unfit for human habitation

Tuesday 3rd: Brownies. Tawney's Warrant Brooch presented to Kay Smart.

Wednesday 4th: Women's Fellowship

Thursday 5th: Half day closing, bell ringing and choir practice

Friday 6th: Guides

Saturday 7th: WOBs at home to Ilminster Town [see programme]

Sunday 8th: Usual services at the places of worship and my 7th birthday.

Monday 9th:

Tuesday 10th: Burial of Harry James Flock, Cave View, 78 years old. My first time at Brownies – I was told I was to be a Gnome!

Wednesday 11th: Women's fellowship

Thursday 12th: Half day, bell ringing and choir practice.

Friday 13th: Guides

Saturday 14th: Grand Coronation Whist Drive at the Church Hall, 7.15 p.m., admission 2/6d

Sunday 1th: Normal services at both Churches

Monday 16^{th:} Wedding of Howell Joshua Davies to Frances Victoria Porter

Tuesday 17th: Brownies

Wednesday 18th: Women's Fellowship

Thursday 19th: Half day closing. Bell ringing and choir practice

Friday 20th: Mercury articles and pictures feature Worle Junior Pageant. Picture with caption 'Arise Sir Walter' must have been taken at a rehearsal. Speculation about a performance in Grove Park.

Saturday 21st:

Sunday 22nd: Usual Church and Chapel services

Monday 23rd:

Tuesday 24th: Estates and Planning Committee approve: a temporary shed on Old Maltings; 10 pairs of semis in Mayfield Avenue; one dwelling in Greenwood Road; a bungalow in Spring Hill; garage at Stepaside, Pine Hill, erection of 4 bungalows at Worle. Decision deferred on a housing estate development at Ebdon Road.

Wednesday 25th: Women's Fellowship

Thursday 26th: Half day closing

Friday 27th: Mr Anderson of Greenwood Road wrote to the Mercury! Schools broke up for Easter for 2 weeks.

Saturday 28th: WOB at home to Watchet Town [programme]

Sunday 29th: Palm Sunday services at Methodist Chapel. St. Martin's 10.00 service includes 12 confirmations of parishioners. See Church records

Monday 30th: Council defer decision of sale of 25 acres at Preanes Green

Tuesday 31st: Brownies

April

Wednesday 1st: Women's fellowship

Thursday 2nd: Burial of Frank Syms, 'St Helens', New Bristol Rd, aged 47

Friday 3rd: Good Friday bank holiday. Service at Methodist Chapel, 11.00 a.m.; St Martin's liturgy from 12 Noon until 3 p.m. Mercury includes a picture of the Railways employees' dinner photograph

Saturday 4th: Early Mist won the Grand National, to Johnnie Tucker's eternal joy

Sunday 5th: Easter Sunday: Services at St. Martins, Holy Eucharist 7.00 a.m. 8.15 and 11.00 [sung]. Solemn Evensong, children's procession and sermon at 3.00.
Worle Methodist services: 11.00 a.m. and 6.30 a.m. Anthem: 'When I Survey'.

Monday 6th: Bank Holiday. Next week's Mercury reports that it rained all day!
WOBs friendly against Old Wulfrunians [see programme]

Tuesday 7th: Brownies

Wednesday 8th: Burial of Eliza Church, 14 Greenwood Road, aged 68

Thursday 9th: Council agree to give money to support the TV showing of the Coronation in the Church Hall for Senior Residents.

Friday 10th: Mercury headline: 'Callous Blasphemy' said Worle Vicar.

Saturday 11th: Coronation Bazaar at Worle Methodist Church

Sunday 12th: Worle Methodist – usual services. St. Martins' 10.00 a.m. service includes Baptisms of Marion Elizabeth Neathway and Stephen Paul Williams.

Monday 13th:

Tuesday 14th: Brownies

Wednesday 15th: Women's fellowship

Thursday 16th: Worle Cricket Club General meeting 8.00 p.m. at the New Inn, attended by 14 members. Broke, so decided not to hold annual dinner. What a shame. Details in Minutes Book.

Friday 17th: Mercury report of St Martin's Church meeting 'Use of Churchyard Path at Worle'
Report of WOBs at home to Easton Rangers

Saturday 18th: Shirley Lickes, Worle's carnival Queen, crowned at the Church Hall.
WOBs v. Bridgwater Town – see programme

Sunday 19th: Services at both Churches at usual times

Monday 20th:

Tuesday 21st: Brownies preparing garden at Church Hall for red, white and blue coronation planting. Seeds handed out to grow at home.

Wednesday 22nd: Women's fellowship

Thursday 23rd: Half day closing, bellringing and choir practice

130

Friday 24th: Mercury announce local council elections to be contested in 5 wards. Mr. Bessell and Mrs Livingstone standing in Milton and Worle. Voting on May 7th.

Saturday 25th: Worle Cricket Club match against Webbington. Score card in cricket book
WOBs at home to Street.

Sunday 26th: Normal services

Monday 27th:

Tuesday 28th: Brownies

Wednesday 30th: Women's fellowship

Thursday 30th: Half day. WOBs v. Taunton, see programme. Draw for free Wembley tickets for four Worle Old Boy members for Cup Final.

May

Friday 1st: Mercury report of W.C.C. success against Webbington: 'Worle opened their season in fine style' .
Burial of James B lock, Green Park, New Bristol Road, aged 80.
Abolition of the colour bar comes into force in time for the Coronation.

Saturday 2nd: F. A. Cup Final at Wembley. Blackpool v. Bolton Wanderers, known as 'The Matthews Final'. R. Rodgers, W. Maggs, M. Herwig and R. Rowlands won the Worle Old Boys' draw for free tickets.

Sunday 3rd: Usual services at both Churches

Monday 4th:

Tuesday 5th: Brownies. Cricket practice at the Rec.

Wednesday 6th: Women's fellowship

Thursday 7th: Half Day closing. Voting for Borough Council Elections today at Worle Junior School, in the building next to the Church now known as Hillside School. See Mercury on 15th for results.

Friday 8th: Cricket practice at the Rec.

Saturday 9th: Worle O. Bs Comic football match for Coronation Funds played on recreation ground.
WCC draw with West Huntspill, see score card in cricket book

Sunday 10th: Normal Church Services.

Monday 11th: Worle Junior School Managers' meeting. Newly elected Mr. Bessell sent apologies!

Tuesday 12th: Brownies.   Cricket practice at the Rec.
Burial of Frederick Charles Carey, aged 77 of Green Park, New Bristol Road, conducted b y Rev Arthur Tuley, Methodist minister. National scarcity of eggs and foodstuffs discussed in Commons. Eggs 5/6 a dozen. To import or not to import? They didn't. Good, we were all right in Worle.

Wednesday 13th:

Thursday 14th: Half day closing. Bell ringing and choir practice.

Friday 15th: Mercury report of Election results. Bessell wins Milton and Worle. Conservatives in complete control of council.
Report of WOBs Comic Football match. Huge success.

Saturday 16th:

Sunday 17th: Usual services. Eggs for breakfast!

Monday 18th:

Tuesday 19th: Brownies

Wednesday 20th: Women's fellowship

Thursday 21st: Half day. Royal Heritage Pageant produced by Worle Junior School in the field behind the Church at 6.00 p.m. Programme and pictures.

Friday 22nd:

Saturday 23rd: Worle Junior School Parent Teachers Association comic cricket match. Photograph

Sunday 24th: Whitsun Sunday. Special services to greet the Holy Ghost Baptism of Mary Lillian Crease of Coronation Road.

Monday 25th: Bank Holiday and the British Legion Carnival. 2.45 from Kewstoke Rd. Sports, prizes, stalls etc and Silver Band on the Rec. Dance in the Marquee in the evening.

Tuesday 26th: Brownies in Church Hall

Wednesday 27th: Women's fellowship. Children's Service for the Queen. 6.45 p.m. in Junior School Playground. Brown Owl's log book records Sue Loud 'first fell up steps, then ran an inch-long splinter into her hand. Dealt with by Tawney Owl.

Thursday 28th: Worle Cricket Club General Meeting in the Pavilion. Was this on the Rec. or behind Nut Tree Farm? Minutes.

Friday 29th: Mercury article – details of coronation day festivities in the district, including Worle.
Carnival exploding car picture. Carnival Queen float picture and caption Burial of Edward John Crocker, Bridge Farm, 79

Saturday 30th: Worle Cricket Club first eleven versus Webbington. Charles 19 not out. Score card

Sunday 31st: Special services for Coronation at St. Martin's and Worle Methodist Chapel.

June

Monday 1st: Chaos escalates on Tripps Field. Animals moved, marquee up, swing boats erected. Children banned. My parents left for London with Lil and Jim Harris to see the Coronation. Town Clerk read out a letter to the Council from Les Bull about putting on the pageant in Grove Park.

Tuesday 2nd: Coronation of H.M. Queen Elizabeth II.
100 older residents of Worle watched the ceremony on Television in the Church Hall. Fair and sports on Tripps Field. 500 Children in marquee for tea and singing. Dance in the evening.

Wednesday 3rd: Children invaded Tripps Field to watch the clearing up. Turned out.
Opening of Commonwealth Conference in London. Queen must have been worn out and fed up, but all the heads of state were already there, so it saved money.

Brownies acted out the Coronation. Elves and Gnomes mimed Prince Philip paying homage; Fairies and Pixies mimed crowning ceremony.

Thursday 4th: Early closing day

Friday 5th: Mercury report of Worle's successful fundraising for Coronation and of the celebrations.

Saturday 6th: Unusual Saturday baptism of Verity Ann Disney and Philip Jeffrey Ham.

Sunday 7th: Services back to normal

Monday 8th: Wedding of Geoffrey Howard Mason to Molly Edwards [Somerset records office, so I hope this unusual Monday wedding date is correct]

Tuesday 9th: Brownies' 15th Anniversary of 1st Worle pack. Civic Defence Committee of Weston Council report on Air Raid Warning Sirens.

Wednesday 10th: Women's fellowship

Thursday 11th: Early closing, bell ringing and choir practice

Friday 12th: Mercury reported the funeral of Jack Hadley, 12 The Rows. RAOB member.
Photo of WOB Football club dance at the Church Hall.

Saturday 13th:

Sunday 14th: Usual services

Monday 15th:

Tuesday 16th: Brownies

Wednesday 17th: Golden Wedding of Herbert Blackmore and Lydia Poole, who were married at St. Martin's Church in 1903 by Preb. A. C. Harman. Pictures, please.

Thursday 18th: Early closing day

Friday 19th: Junior School outing to Stratford-upon-Avon. See picture and note.
Picture in Mercury of the fire at Skid's storage garage on Mendip Avenue. WOB dance picture and caption in Mercury

Saturday 20th.

Sunday 21st: Worle Methodist: usual services. St Martin's: morning service included the baptism of Janet Mary Rodger.

Monday 22nd:

Tuesday 23rd: Brownies' Owl Hunt in Vicarage Garden for midsummer.

Wednesday 24th: Burial of Albert Henry Heard, 21 Church Road, 67

Thursday 25th: WCC first eleven played at Webbington. Score Card. Worle Junior School paid A. Butcher, secretary of Bath and Wells insurance board 7/- in respect of legal liability insurance for accidents.

Friday 26th: Worle man, Charles Nutt, cleared of stealing a vice from RAF Locking.
Mercury reports that 'Rate Rise is Last Straw'.

Saturday 27th:

Sunday 28th: Normal Sabbath

Monday 29th:

Tuesday 30th:

July

Wednesday 1st: Women's fellowship

Thursday 2nd: Half day closing, Bell ringing and choir practice

Friday 3rd: Mercury report of WCC match against Wells. No score card but Mercury says Worle 106, Wells 77.
Burial of Alice Elizabeth Rice, Town House, Worle

Saturday 4th: Worle Junior School Royal Heritage Pageant performance in Grove Park

Sunday 5th: Normal services

Monday 6th:

Tuesday 7th: Brownies

Wednesday 8th: Housing committee discussed temporary bungalows at Worle and a place to keep street decorations from the Coronation. Nowhere found! It is not known what happened to them.   Land for housing at Worle. Purchase of sites discussed.

Thursday 9th: Parks, parades and sands committee discussed Lobby Lud, the man who walked the seafront waiting to be spotted by tourists carrying the right newspaper.

Friday 10th: Mercury picture of Worle Junior School Pageant. Caption 'still smiling' is a reference to the pouring rain.
Report in the paper of Worle Evening Institute, an offshoot of the College [The Tech].
Worle Cricket Club beat Axbridge by 55 runs.

Saturday 11th: Charles Bennett and Brenda Groves married at St. Martin's. Report in Mercury of 17th July.

Sunday 12th: Usual services at Church and Chapel

Monday 13th:

Tuesday 14th: Brownies

Wednesday 15th: Women's fellowship.
Burial of Conningsby Guthrie Tindall Nicholson of West Wick, aged 68

Thursday 16th:

Friday 17th: Schools broke up for the Summer Holiday.
Mercury reports of Brian Disney's head injury and of Sandra Gill
being knocked down by a motor cyclist.

Saturday 18th: Weddings of: Charles
William Bennett and Brenda Ellen Groves and
Valentine Beacham and Margaret Knight

Sunday 19th: Usual Church and Chapel services

Monday 20th:

Tuesday 21st: Brownies

Wednesday 22nd: Rent paid by headmaster to Worle Junior School
account £6/5/-

Thursday 23rd: Half day closing

Friday 24th: Mercury report of Arthur Eames of Old Bristol Road
being injured in a road accident.

Saturday 25th: Wedding of Geoffrey Hawkins to Margaret Venning
of Coronation Road.

Sunday 26th:

Monday 27th:

Tuesday 28th:

Wednesday 29th: Burial of Harold Arthur Herring, Greenwood
Road, aged 58

Thursday 30th:

Friday 31st: Worle Junior School Managers' meeting. Only 4
attended!

August

Saturday 1st: A. J. Beakes, Lawrence Road, married Bessie R. Coles, Kirklands, High St.
Robert Bale married Brenda Andrews, 99 Church Road,

Sunday 2nd: St. Martins morning service included the baptism of Avril Jane Richards, Greenwood Rd, who was 7 years old.

Monday 3rd: August Bank Holiday. Worle Flower Show. Sweet Peas back on top. The day the Cricket Club tea things disappeared.

Tuesday 4th:

Wednesday 5th: Council approve a Skittle Alley for Lamb Inn, a bungalow in Ebdon Road and 5 other applications for Worle.

Thursday 6th: Half day closing

Friday 7th: Long report of Flower show in Mercury, reflecting its importance in the area.

Saturday 8th:

Sunday 9th: Pauline Elizabeth Disney baptised at St. Martin's

Monday 10th: Everything stopped to complete the harvest. Factories on 2 weeks annual holiday.

Tuesday 11th:

Wednesday 12th:

Thursday 13th:

Friday 14th:

Saturday 15th:

Sunday 16th: Church and Chapel, as usual

Monday 17th:

Tuesday 18th:

Wednesday 19th:

Thursday 20th:

Friday 21st:

Saturday 22nd: Back to life! Wedding of Ray and June Ackland at Saviour's Church. Ray was born at New Cottage, the Scaurs.

Sunday 23rd: Normal Church and Chapel services

Monday 24th: Burial of Herbert George Church, 14 Greenwood Road, aged 57

Tuesday 25th:

Wednesday 26th:

Thursday 27th:

Friday 28th: Report of death of H.G. Church who had farmed until he retired, at Grapevine Farm, St. Georges.

Saturday 29th: New football season started. WOB at home to Street, Reserves home to Minehead. See programme.
WJ School paid Somerset River Board 12/-
British Legion Sale of Work.

Sunday 30th: Usual services

Monday 31st: Schools re-open after Summer break. See WJS register detailing new intake.
Council discussed SWEB's transformer on Recreation Ground.

September

Tuesday 1ˢᵗ: Brownies welcomed 3 'tweenies', Margaret Bray, Sally Bowditch and Raye Jones.

Wednesday 2ⁿᵈ: Women's fellowship

Thursday 3ʳᵈ: Early closing

Friday 4ᵗʰ: Long Mercury reports about Worle Old Boys for the new season. Minehead game and new signings. Game against Street in the Somerset Senior League and fixtures for the season.
Worle British Legion Sale of Work report.
Worle Cricket Club committee meeting: stiff letter to horticultural committee about the missing tea things.

Saturday 5ᵗʰ: WOB v. Street, programme. Worle played in Red and White for this match.

Sunday 6ᵗʰ: Worle Methodist Chapel Harvest Festival Services.

Monday 7ᵗʰ: Harvest Supper at Methodist Church Hall, followed by a Dutch auction of produce conducted by Mr. Sievewright.

Tuesday 8ᵗʰ: Brownies

Wednesday 9ᵗʰ: Women's fellowship

Thursday 10ᵗʰ:

Friday 11ᵗʰ:

Saturday 12ᵗʰ: WOB away to Wells City
Shirley Margaret Angela Vaughan married Maurice Reginald Bryant. See pictures and account of the small bridesmaid who missed the picnic.   Brownies' picnic to Uphill Sands. Bus from the New Inn. Take bus fare for both ways and tea in a satchel. Home by 7.00 p.m.

141

Sunday 13th: Usual services

Monday 14th:

Tuesday 15th:

Wednesday 16th: Women's fellowship

Thursday 17th: Half day closing, bellringing and choir practice.

Friday 18th: Mercury report: WOB 3-0 win over Wells City.

Saturday 19th: WOB at home to Hanham in the Amateur Cup, Programme.

Sunday 20th: Usual services

Monday 21st: Wedding of Albert Henry Borwick to Margaret Lilian Diamond, both of 'The Nurseries' Kewstoke Road.

Tuesday 22nd: Brownies

Wednesday 23rd:

Thursday 24th:

Friday 25th:

Saturday 26th: WOB away to Odd Down.
Joyce Edwards married Jim House.

Sunday 27th: Harvest Festival services at St. Martin's. The first High Celebration of the Holy Eucharist since the reformation. Full Mercury report on 2nd Oct.

Monday 28th: Burial of Edmund John Phillips, 4 Preanes Green, aged 34.

Tuesday 29th: Borough Council Estates and Planning refused permission for a caravan park at Meadows, Ebdon Road.

Wednesday 30th:

October

Thursday 1st: Worle Junior's Ecclesiastical Insurance £1.13.3d. Head's contribution 5/-.

Friday 2nd: Mercury report of special services at St. Martin's. Report of Joyce Edwards' wedding to Jim House

Saturday 3rd: WOBs home to Glastonbury, see programme

Sunday 4th: St. Martin's morning service included baptisms of Carolyn Mary Deal of 'Hillside' Worle and David Nicholas Petty, 85 Church Road.

Monday 5th: Housing Committee meeting decided to appropriate land at Preanes Green.

Tuesday 6th: Brownies

Wednesday 7th:

Thursday 8th: Half day and bell practice

Friday 9th:

Saturday 10th: WOB away to High Littleton.
Burial of William Robert Anderson, Greenwood Road, aged 72

Sunday 11th: Worle Methodist Chapel anniversary services today. Choir sang 'Oh Lord how Manifold' anthem. Children sang solas, duets and recited. Short sermon. Good fun.

Monday 12th:

Tuesday 13th:

Wednesday 14th:

Thursday 15th: Half day and wedding of Edward House to Millicent Edwards, Laurel Farm.

Friday 16th: Report of Milton and Worle Townswomen's Guild meeting [Toc H Hall, Milton] to decide programme for 1954.

Saturday 17th: WOBs at home to Odd Down

Sunday 18th: Usual services.

Monday 19th:

Tuesday 20th: Burial of Florence Emily Kingsbury, 68 of Lyefield Farm Brownies' Road Safety week.

Wednesday 21st:

Thursday 22nd:

Friday 23rd: Mercury report of Worle Colllision between van and motor cyclist. Huish and George in van. Lacey on bike.
Report of Florence Kingsbury's funeral.
Worle Cricket Club meeting at New Inn. Joyce's wedding present discussed. See minutes.

Saturday 24th: WOBs away to Taunton Town

Sunday 25th: Usual services

Monday 26th: Worle Junior School's managers meeting. Only 4 attended again. No Mr. Bessell, of course.

Tuesday 27th: Estates and Planning meeting proposed widening of High Street/Scaurs junction.
Brownies: enrolment of Margaret Bray, Sally Bowditch and Raye Green. Mothers attended [Fathers not invited].

Wednesday 28th: Public Health and Water council meeting: Burning of offal at Forces factory discussed, but not by name, referred to as 'at certain premises'.

Thursday 29th:

Friday 30th:

Saturday 31st: WOB home to Frome Town, programme.
W J School received rent of £6/5/- form Mr. Bull for school house.
Townswomen's Guild whist drive at Toc H Hall.

November

Sunday 1st: Usual services

Monday 2nd: Housing committee meeting: Effluent and sewage at Preanes Green

Tuesday 3rd: Worle Cricket Club Annual General Meeting at New Inn. Election of Officers.

Wednesday 4th:

Thursday 5th: Fireworks in the lane off greenwood Road. Guy Fawkes all over the High Street. Bonfire on Tripps' Field.

Friday 6th: Mercury: complaint of Obnoxious Smells. From Ratepayers' Association. They also asked for the 'removal of the bottleneck' at the bus terminus.

Saturday 7th: WOB away to Highbridge Town

Sunday 8th: Usual Services

Monday 9th:

Tuesday 10th: Brownies: competition for the best written report of Princess Margaret's visit to be delivered to Nora Jefferies' house by 16th of the month. Prayers said by Brown Owl and Jenny Vaughan.

Wednesday 11th:

Thursday 12th:

Friday 13th: Golden Wedding report of Mr. and Mrs. Griffin, Elm Cottage. See photo of cycle shop.

Saturday 14th: WOBs at home to Ilminster Town, programme. Church Bazaar in Church Hall.

Sunday 15th: Remembrance Sunday services in Churches and at the War Memorial. Baptism of Corrine Marilyn Morris, 4 High Street.

Monday 16th:

Tuesday 17th: Brownies held at the Junior School today. Brown Owl conducted a 'Stop, look and listen' walk to the village and back.

Wednesday 18th:

Thursday 19th:

Worle Vicar and 'Finest Tribute' report of Remembrance Sunday Services WOB beat Highbridge 8 – 1. Long report.
St Martin's Bazaar picture and report.

Saturday 21st: WOB reserves away to Locking.
WOB 1st Eleven at home to Ilminster. Programme.

Sunday 22nd: Usual services

Monday 23rd: Council meeting discussed the smell at Worle!

Tuesday 24th:

Wednesday 25th: Women's Fellowship

Thursday 26th: Half day and bell practice

Friday 27th: 'Sweeten Worle's Atmosphere' headline in paper and report of council discussions.

Saturday 28th: WOBs away to Bridgwater Town

Sunday 29th: Usual services.

Monday 30th:

December

Tuesday 1st: Estates and Planning meeting: Land at Station Road belonging to Weston, Clevedon and Portishead Light Railway acquired.

Wednesday 2nd:

Thursday 3rd:

Friday 4th:

Saturday 5th: WOBs away to Chard Town, programme

Sunday 6th: Usual services

Monday 7th:

Tuesday 8th:

Wednesday 9th:

Thursday 10th: Worle Junior School –emergency managers' meeting to consider applications for post of Assistant master. Burial of Oliver Tucker, Ebdon Road, aged 51.

Friday 11th: Mercury report of cyclist without lights in High Street. Times and nature of Christmas services at St. Martin's announced.

Saturday 12th:

Sunday 13th:

Monday 14th: Johnnie Mayled involved in fatal road accident near Annandale Avenue.

Tuesday 15th: Worle Junior School paid £10 expenses to S. Gibbins, the correspondent.

Wednesday 16th:

Thursday 17th:

Friday 18th: Burial Service for John Mayled at St. Martin's. Mercury report of assessment of Worle bungalow for rating purposes and a report of the death of John Mayled.

Saturday 19th: WOBs away to Glastonbury. Wedding of Derek Matthew to Jeanne J'Anson, The Garth, Worle.

Sunday 20th: Usual services. St Martin's morning service included the baptism of Pamela Jan Lucas.

Monday 21st: Worle Junior School managers met at the Vicarage at 2.30 p.m. to interview 2 candidates for a teaching post. Terry Jones was appointed.

Tuesday 22nd: Brown Owl's report on the year. 'We are very pleased with our Brownies. They have worked well and have a wonderful pack spirit'. It refers to a scrapbook of World Brownies made during the year.

Wednesday 23rd:

Thursday 24th: Fine day. Everyone shopping in High Street. Lights on. 11.30 p.m. – blessing of the crib and midnight mass at St. Martin's.

Friday 25th: 8.00 a.m. Holy Eucharist. 12.15 p.m. Holy Eucharist. 11.00 a.m. Matins and Sermon.

Saturday 26th: WOB organised a special testimonial match on this day against Bourneville in memory of John Mayled. Programme

Sunday 27th: Preacher at St. Martin's: Mr. P. Jones

Monday 28th: Burial of Christopher Radford, Coronation Road, aged 75

Tuesday 29th: Worle Junior School expenditure: Alice Coles Charity – Way leave 1/-.
Council Estates and Planning committee approved 4 building projects in Worle.

Wednesday 30th:

Thursday 31st: Ebenezer Methodist Chapel Social evening at 8.00 p.m. in the schoolroom, and Watchnight Service at 11.30 p.m. in the Chapel.

And suddenly, it's 1954.

Cover picture: Worle High Street, under a blanket of snow in 1953.
Manor House Farm, gas lamp standards, trees at the bottom of
Spring Hill. Lovely.

For my children and their children, with my love.